A COLLECTION OF PERFORMANCE TASKS AND RUBRICS:

UPPER ELEMENTARY SCHOOL MATHEMATICS

Charlotte Danielson

EYE ON EDUCATION
6 DEPOT WAY WEST, SUITE 106
LARCHMONT, NY 10538
(914) 833-0551 phone
(914) 833-0761 fax

Library of Congress Cataloging-in-Publication Data

Danielson, Charlotte.
    A collection of performance tasks and rubrics : upper elementary
school mathematics / Charlotte Danielson.
        p.   cm.
    ISBN 1-883001-39-0
    1. Mathematics--Study and teaching (Elementary)--Evaluation.
I. Title.
QA135.5.D245   1997
372.7--dc21   97-10141
                                                                   CIP

PRINTED IN CANADA

ABOUT THE AUTHOR

Charlotte Danielson is President of Princeton Education Associates in Princeton, New Jersey and Senior Associate for Assessment for the Council for Basic Education in Washington, DC. She has worked as a consultant on performance assessment for numerous schools and school districts in the United States and overseas, and has designed materials and training programs for ASCD and ETS. Her work has encouraged assessment in the service of learning by both teachers and students. Recent publications include *Enhancing Professional Practice: A Framework for Teaching*, the Professional Inquiry Kit *Teaching for Understanding*, both published by ASCD, and *A Collection of Performance Tasks and Rubrics: Middle School Mathematics*.

ACKNOWLEDGMENTS

The author would like to thank Barbara Smith, Mathematics Supervisor of the Unionville-Chadds Ford School District and Donna Schore of Murray Elementary School in Larchmont, NY for contributing student work samples to several of the tasks. Special thanks are also due to New Standards™, the State Departments of Education of California, Connecticut, Kentucky, Oregon and Vermont, and the National Academy Press for granting permission for re-printing several of the tasks developed under their auspices.

School Supplies, Science Fair, and Spinners were reprinted with permission from New Standards™. The New Standards™ assessment system includes performance standards with performance descriptions, student work samples and commentaries, on-demand examinations, and a portfolio system. For more information, contact the National Center on Education and the Economy, 202-783-3668 or http://www.ncee.org.

TABLE OF CONTENTS

FOREWORD

The *Curriculum and Evaluation Standards for School Mathematics* released by the National Council of Teachers of Mathematics (NCTM) have profoundly influenced the vision and practice of mathematics education. Through their call for a greater emphasis on problem solving, reasoning, and communications, the *Standards* have validated the expanded use of performance tasks for classroom instruction and assessment. Effective performance tasks call for such reasoning and communication by engaging students in applying mathematical concepts and skills in the context of "authentic" problems.

While educators generally understand and support the recommendations of NCTM to incorporate performance tasks for assessment purposes, a number of practical questions remain – how do teachers develop "authentic" tasks to assess students' understanding, reasoning and mathematical communication?; how does the use of performance tasks fit with more traditional forms of assessment in mathematics?; how do teachers evaluate student responses since performance tasks typically call for more than a single, correct answer?

Charlotte Danielson offers timely and practical answers in this readable guide to the development and use of performance tasks and rubrics in upper elementary school classrooms. The book provides an excellent overview of the rationale for, and the strengths and limitations of, the use of performance tasks to assess student achievement and progress in mathematics. She offers a user-friendly, field-tested process for developing performance tasks and rubrics,

along with practical advice for evaluating student work, selecting "anchors", and establishing performance standards.
Finally, the sample tasks, rubrics and student work samples
provide "tried and true" resources for immediate use, while
serving as models to guide development of additional tasks
and scoring tools.

Readers of *A Collection of Performance Tasks and Rubrics* will
not be confronted with an "ivory tower" treatise on what
should be. Rather, they will discover a valuable resource,
grounded in the wisdom of years of experience in schools and
classrooms, for making the NCTM vision come to life.

— Jay McTighe
Director, Maryland Assessment Consortium

PREFACE

Educators have recognized for some time the unique role of assessment in the classroom environment. Assessment provides valuable information for both teachers and students regarding how well everyone is doing. Students can see where they went wrong in their understanding; and teachers can determine whether a concept needs to be re-taught. This function, of monitoring progress on valued learning goals, is the first purpose of assessment, and one that supports every other purpose.

Assessment also defines what students must know and be able to do to succeed in a particular teacher's class; students frequently say that they don't know, until they have seen a teacher's first tests in the fall, just what that person values. Is this person a stickler for details? Or are the big ideas all that is important? When teachers coach their students in how to prepare for a test, they are conveying what is important, both to them and in the subject. Such coaching can serve a clarifying purpose for teachers as well as students; by specifying what their students should study in preparation for a test, and in designing that test, teachers must confront their subject and make decisions about what is truly important.

However, there is much more to assessment than simply monitoring of student progress and clarifying expectations. Because most tests "count," they motivate as well. That is, to the extent that tests or other assessments are used to calculate students' grades, students will try to do well. Tests can "count" for teachers as well. In some towns, for example, scores on standardized tests are published in the newspaper; student scores on AP tests are seen as reflections on their teachers' instructional skills; and some states and school districts use test scores as the basis for rewards or sanctions. When test scores matter, teachers will attempt to have their students do well. And while few teachers will engage in unethical practices, most teachers will provide instruction in such a manner as to assist their students in performing as well as they can.

But it is not only in defining the content that tests and other assessments influence practice. The form matters as well. That is, when students are asked on tests (and know in advance that they will be asked) to answer a number of multiple-choice or short-answer questions, they tend to prepare in that manner, committing to memory that which they predict will be on the test. If deeper understanding is not required for the test, they may not strive to achieve it. If a question is ambiguous, they will seek to "read the mind" of the teacher, to determine the right answer even if they believe another is better.

The form of assessments also affects teachers' practices. If a test does not require, or does not reward, understanding, why should teachers emphasize it in their own classrooms? If all that is needed in mathematics, for example, is for students to get the right answer (possibly without understanding why the procedure works) then the procedure is all that will be provided in some classrooms.

Assessments matter, therefore, both in what they assess and how they assess it. The content of a test affects what students study and teachers teach, and the form of the assessment affects how they approach the task. Teachers have discovered, for example, that if they want their students to become better writers, they must make good writing count in the classroom; they must teach it systematically and assess it authentically. A test of correcting errors, for example, will not do; they must assess students' actual writing. Similarly, if teachers want students to acquire skills in solving mathematical problems, or communicating their mathematical ideas, they must both teach and assess those skills.

These considerations have provided much of the energy behind the movement towards "performance assessment," that is, students actually creating or constructing an answer to a question. Teachers and policy-makers alike have discovered that when assessment tasks more accurately mirror the types of learning goals they have for students -- both in the content and the form of assessment -- the learning environment is transformed. The assessments themselves tend to be motivational and engaging; students invest energy in the tasks and commit to them. In addition, performance assessments even serve to educate as well as assess student learning; teachers find that their students learn from doing performance tasks.

However, performance assessment has one enormous drawback; it is time-consuming to do, both to design and to work into classroom instructional time. Even teachers who are committed to the practice of performance assessment find that they don't have time to design good performance tasks, to try them out with students, and perfect them for later use. Furthermore, most teachers did not learn to design performance tasks and scoring rubrics as part of their professional preparation. And while many educators have learned such skills as part of their continuing professional growth, they may lack the confidence to use such performance tasks as a central part of their assessment plan.

This book is designed to address this need. It is based on the assumption that many educators are interested in incorporating performance assessment into their classroom routines, but have either not yet acquired the technical skill or do not have the time required to design them on their own. This book provides a collection of performance tasks and scoring rubrics for a number of topics in upper elementary school mathematics, which teachers can use as is, or adapt for their students and their particular situation. It is intended to save time for busy educators, to provide examples of tested performance tasks. The samples of student work provide a range of responses, to clarify the tasks, and to anchor the points on the scoring rubrics.

Chapter One provides the reader with an introduction to performance assessment and how it is distinguished from traditional testing. Chapter Two offers a rationale for performance assessment, explaining its strengths (and its drawbacks) as compared with more traditional approaches. In Chapter Three the reader can find guidance in making an evaluation plan, and linking that plan to the overall approach to curriculum development. Chapter Four consists of an overview of evaluating complex performance, and includes a description of evaluating non-school (and yet complex) performance that can be used in a workshop setting to introduce educators to performance assessment. Chapters Five and Six offer a step-by-step procedure for creating a performance task and a rubric for classroom use, while Chapter Seven suggests techniques for adapting an existing performance task for use in one's own classroom. Chapter Eight is the heart of the collection, and offers performance tasks (some with samples of student work) and rubrics, covering the major topics in upper elementary school mathematics, designed to be adapted, or used as is, in your classroom. The Appendix contains handouts of each of the 24 tasks which may be photocopied and distributed to students.

1

INTRODUCTION

This book concerns the classroom use of performance assessment, and the evaluation of student work in response to performance tasks. It contains a collection of performance tasks in upper elementary school mathematics, but also includes guidance for educators to design or adapt performance tasks for their own use.

While performance assessment is essential to a well-rounded assessment plan, it should not be used exclusively. Traditional testing has an important role to play, particularly in assessing a large domain or evaluating student knowledge. But in assessing student understanding, in order to ascertain how well students can apply their knowledge, some type of performance assessment is essential.

In this book, performance assessment means any assessment of student learning that requires the evaluation of student writing, products, or behavior. That is, it includes all assessment with the exception of multiple choice, matching, true/false testing, or problems with a single correct answer. Classroom-based performance assessment includes all such assessment that occurs in the classroom and is evaluated by teachers as distinct from large-scale, state-wide performance testing programs.

Performance assessment is fundamentally criterion-referenced rather than norm-referenced. That is, teachers who adopt performance assessment are concerned with the degree to which students can demonstrate knowledge and skill in a certain field. They know what it means to demonstrate competence; the purpose of a performance assessment is to allow students to show what they can do. The criteria for evaluating performance are important; teachers use their professional judgment in establishing such criteria and defining levels of performance. And the standards they set for student performance are typically above that expected for minimal competency; they define accomplished performance.

Norm-referenced tests are less valuable to teachers than are performance assessments. True, teachers may learn what their students can do compared to other students of the same age. However, the items on the test may or may not reflect the curriculum of a given school or district; to the extent that these are different, the information provided may not be of value to the teacher. Moreover, the results of most standardized tests are not known for some time. Even for those items included in a school's curriculum, it does not help a teacher to know in June, that a student did not know, in April, a concept that was taught the previous November. Of what possible use is that information to the teacher in June? It may not even still be true. And even if true, the information comes too late to be useful.

In addition, the only way students demonstrate progress on a norm-referenced test is in comparison to other students. Progress *per se* is not shown as progress. That is, a student's standing may move from the 48th percentile to the 53rd percentile. However, the student may not have learned much but other students may have learned less! So while norm-referenced tests have their value, for example for large-scale program evaluation, they are of limited use to teachers who want to know what their students have learned. Performance assessment, then, is criterion-referenced. It reflects the curriculum goals of a teacher, school, or district, and when used in the context of classroom teaching, it informs instructional decisions. In the remaining sections of this chapter, the different uses and types of performance assessment are described.

SUMMARY

Classroom based performance assessment is criterion-referenced and is used to evaluate student learning on clearly identified instructional goals. As such, it should be designed to be of optimal usefulness to its different audiences: teachers, students, and parents.

THE USES OF CLASSROOM-BASED PERFORMANCE ASSESSMENT

Assessment of student learning in the classroom is done for many purposes and can serve many ends. When teachers design their assessment strategies, it is helpful to determine, at the outset, which of the many possible uses they have in mind. Some possibilities are described here.

INSTRUCTIONAL DECISION-MAKING

Many teachers discover, after they have taught a concept, that many students didn't "get it;" that, while they may have had looks of understanding on their faces, and may have participated in the instructional activities, they are unable to demonstrate the knowledge or understanding on their own.

This is important information for teachers to have, as they determine what to do next with a class, or even with a few students. They may decide that they must re-teach the concept, or create a different type of instructional activity. Alternatively, if only a few students lack understanding, a teacher might decide to work with them separately, or to design an activity which can be used for peer tutoring.

Whatever course of action a teacher decides upon, however, it is decided on the basis of information regarding student understanding. That implies that the assessment strategies used will reveal student understanding, or lack of it. And when used for instructional decision-making, it is the teacher alone who uses the information. The results of the assessment are not shared with students, nor are they used for grading. The assessment is solely for the teacher's benefit, to determine whether the instructional activities achieved their intended purpose.

FEEDBACK TO STUDENTS

Performance assessment, like any assessment, may also be used to provide feedback to students regarding their progress. Depending on how it is constructed, a performance task can let students know in which dimensions of performance they excel, and in which they need to devote additional energy. Such feedback is, by its nature, individualized; the feedback provided to one student will be very different from that provided to another if their performances are different. It is efficient for the teacher, however, since the important dimensions of performance have been identified beforehand.

COMMUNICATION WITH PARENTS

Actual student performance on well-designed tasks can provide parents with authentic evidence of their child's level of functioning. Many parents are skeptical of tests which they don't understand, and are not sure of the meaning of numbers, percentiles and scalene scores. But student answers to an open-ended question are easy to understand and can serve to demonstrate to parents the level of performance of their child. These samples of student work are highly beneficial for open house or parent conferences, to validate the judgments of the teacher.

Such indication of student performance is of particular importance if a teacher is concerned about a child and wants to persuade a parent that action is needed. It is impossible for parents, when confronted with the work of their own child, to question the commitment of the teacher in meeting that child's needs. Whether the work is exemplary and the teacher is recommending a more advanced placement, or the work reveals poor understanding, the actual samples of student performance are invaluable to a teacher in making a case for action.

SUMMATIVE EVALUATION OF STUDENT LEARNING

Like any assessment strategy, a performance assessment may be used to evaluate student learning and may contribute to decisions regarding grades. The issue of grading is complex and will be addressed more fully on page 19 of this book, but the results from performance tasks, like any assessment, can serve to substantiate a teacher's judgment in assigning a grade.

SUMMARY

Classroom-based assessment may be used for several different purposes. An overall assessment plan will take all desired purposes into account.

DIFFERENT TYPES OF CLASSROOM-BASED ASSESSMENT

Assessment takes many forms, depending on the types of instructional goals being assessed, and the use to which the assessment will be put. The major types are presented in table form, and are described below.

TESTS

Tests are listed as the first major column in Figure 1.1. They have always been (and will continue to be) an important method for ascertaining what students know and can do. When teachers decide to move to more authentic aspects of performance in order to evaluate student learning, they do not abandon tests. On the contrary, they use tests for those types of assessment for which they are well suited (for example, for sampling knowledge), recognizing their substantial strengths as a methodology.

Tests are generally given to students under what we call "testing conditions," that is, conditions that ensure that we are actually getting the authentic work of individuals and that the experience is the same for all students. Testing conditions are:

- *Limited time.* Generally speaking, time for a test is strictly limited. Students must complete the test within a certain amount of time (frequently a class period, but sometimes

FIGURE 1.1 FORMS OF ASSESSMENT

TEST		PRODUCT		BEHAVIOR	
Multiple Choice	Constructed Response	Written	Physical	Structured	Spontaneous

Adapted from a worksheet developed by the Maryland Assessment Consortium.

more or less than that.) This provision ensures that some students don't devote far greater time to the assignments than others.

- *Limited (or no) resources.* Although there are exceptions to this rule (such as open-book tests), students taking a test are usually not permitted to consult materials as they work. An insistence on no additional resources rules out, of course, trips to the library while taking a test. This provision ensures that what students produce on the test reflects only their own understanding.

- *No talking with peers or looking on others' papers.* When taking a test, it is important that students produce their own work. Unless teachers adhere to this condition, they are never sure whether what they receive from an individual student reflects that student's understanding, or that of his or her friends.

In addition, tests are of two basic types: Select and Constructed-response.

- *Multiple choice.* In a multiple-choice test, students select the best answer from those given. True/false and matching tests may also be included in this category. Short-answer items are technically constructed response items (since the student supplies the answer), but since there is generally a single right answer, such items are a special case, and share more characteristics in their scoring with multiple-choice items.

- *Constructed-response.* In a constructed-response test, students answer a question in their own words. Open-ended questions are constructed response, as are essay questions on a test.

Of course, a single test may contain a combination of multiple-choice and constructed-response items. In fact, most tests do; they generally consist of some multiple-choice, true/false, short-answer, or matching items for a portion of the test and several essays for the remainder. The balance between these different types of test items varies enormously, by subject, grade level, and the preference of the teacher.

PRODUCT

A product is any item produced by students which is evaluated according to established criteria. A product is a thing, a physical object, and is generally (but not always) produced by students outside of school time. Students may take as long as they want and need to, and may consult books and speak with other people. Products may be one of two types: written or physical.

- *Written products.* A written product may be a term paper, an essay for homework, a journal entry, a drama, or a lab report. It is anything written by students, but not under testing conditions.

- *Physical products.* A physical product may be, for example, a diorama, a science construction, a project in industrial arts, or a sculpture. Physical products are three-dimensional things, and take up space.

Some projects done by students represent a combination of written and physical products. For example, most science fair projects consist of a physical construction of some sort, combined with a written description of the scientific principles involved.

Products are a rich source of information for teachers in seeking to understand what their students know and can do. However, they have a significant disadvantage, which limits their usefulness for high-stakes assessment. This relates to authenticity. When a student turns in a project, the teacher has no way of knowing the degree to which the work reflects the student's own knowledge and understanding, and the degree to which the student's parents or older siblings might have assisted.

For instructional purposes, most teachers encourage their students to obtain as much help as they can get; students are bound to learn more from an assignment with the insights of additional people. However, for purposes of assessment we need to know what each student can do; this requirement limits the usefulness of out-of-class assignments for evaluation. When used, they should be supplemented by other sources of information (for example, an assignment given under testing conditions) of which the teacher can be sure of authorship.

BEHAVIOR

Lastly, students demonstrate their knowledge or skill through their behavior, and this behavior can be evaluated. Behavior is that aspect of student performance which does not result in a tangible object; once completed, it is finished. However, behavior may be captured and stored, and then evaluated. For example, a skit may be videotaped, or a student reading aloud may be audiotaped. There are two types of behavior which may be used for evaluation:

- *Structured behavior.* In structured behavior, students are performing according to a pre-established framework. They may be staging a debate or a panel discussion. They may be giving a skit, performing a dance, or making a presentation. Teachers may be interviewing their students. Drama and speech classes depend on this type of performance to evaluate learning; it is useful in other fields as well. In virtually every state, acquiring a driver's license depends on successful performance behind the wheel.

- *Spontaneous behavior.* Students can also reveal their understanding through their spontaneous behavior. For example, their interaction when working on group projects, their questions during a discussion and their choices during free time, all demonstrate important aspects of their learning.

Because of the unstructured nature of spontaneous behavior, it is useful primarily as a supplemental form of assessment. However, for certain types of instructional goals, such as skill in collaboration, it may be the only appropriate form. The documentation of spontaneous behavior depends on careful observation. Many teachers use checklists so they can make their "kid watching" as systematic as possible.

SUMMARY

There are different types of classroom assessment. The major types include tests, products, and behavior. Depending on the types of instructional goals to be assessed, they are all valuable. For the purposes of this book all assessment except multiple-choice tests are considered performance assessment.

2

WHY PERFORMANCE ASSESSMENT?

It is clear that the design and implementation of performance assessment are far more time-consuming than the use of traditional tests. Why, one might ask, should a busy educator go to the trouble of changing? A good question, and one that deserves a thoughtful answer.

First, it should be made clear that when teachers use performance assessment, they don't stop using traditional forms of assessment. Tests will always be with us, and they should be. It is frequently important to ascertain what students know about a subject; alternatively, we must be sure that they have read an assignment. There is no substitute for a quiz or a test to ascertain these things. But as a steady diet, tests have serious limitations. These are described below.

THE LIMITATIONS OF TRADITIONAL TESTING

When we refer to "traditional testing" in this book, we mean multiple-choice, true/false, matching, or short-answer tests that teachers create or adapt for use in their classrooms. These are generally provided by the publishers of text programs, or have evolved over time. As noted above, they are useful for certain purposes (and they are certainly efficient to score), but when used exclusively, they have a negative influence.

VALIDITY

The most serious criticism of traditional tests is that the

range of student knowledge and skill that can be tested is extremely limited. Many aspects of understanding to which teachers and their communities are most committed simply don't lend themselves to multiple-choice assessment. To illustrate this point, it is helpful to identify the different categories of educational purposes (instructional goals) and to consider how they can be assessed.

There are, of course, many different ways to classify goals for this type of analysis; one comprehensive classification scheme is outlined below

- *Knowledge.* Most types of knowledge, whether procedural knowledge (i.e., how to wash lab equipment), conceptual understanding (i.e., the meaning of buoyancy), and the application of knowledge (i.e., determining the amount of paint needed to paint a room), may all be assessed through traditional means. Indeed, it is in the assessment of knowledge that traditional assessment rightfully exerts its strongest influence.

  Conceptual understanding, however, is not ideally suited to traditional testing since students can memorize, for example, a definition of "buoyancy" without really understanding it; their lack of understanding might not be revealed through a multiple-choice or matching test. It is only through their explanation of the concept in their own words, or their use of the concept in a problem that their understanding, or lack of it, is demonstrated.

- *Reasoning.* Traditional testing is poorly suited to the assessment of reasoning. While it is true that well-designed multiple-choice tests may be used to evaluate pure logic, most teachers without technical skills in this area are not advised to attempt it. Most of the reasoning we care about in schools (i.e., analyzing data, formulating and testing hypotheses, recognizing patterns) is better assessed through alternative means.

- *Communication.* In order to know whether students can

communicate, we must ask them to do so in writing or speaking. Attempts are made, of course, to evaluate students' understanding of written text and spoken language through multiple-choice tests. To some extent these attempts are successful but they rarely give teachers information they did not already have through more informal means. For the productive aspects of communication — writing and speaking — there is no substitute for students actually writing and speaking, and then evaluating their performance.

• *Skills*. Social skills and psychomotor skills are completely unsuited to traditional forms of assessment. A multiple-choice test on the rules of basketball does not tell a teacher whether or not a student can dribble the ball. And a matching test on how to work in groups does not convey whether students have actually acquired skills in collaboration. Nothing short of observation will do, using a carefully prepared observation guide. To the extent that skills are important aspects of learning, teachers must employ non-traditional assessment methods.

• *Affective Areas*. As with skills, traditional testing is entirely unsuited to the assessment of the affective domain. To the extent that teachers attempt to cultivate students' productive dispositions towards work (e.g., an open mind, pride in a job well done) they must look for little indicators through student behavior. As teachers try to cultivate an aesthetic sense in their students, for example appreciation of the mood of a poem, or the patterns in the multiplication tables, they must look for little comments and signs from their students. Other aspects of the affective domain are equally ill-matched to traditional testing, from self-confidence, to traits such as honesty and respect for private property, through the ability to weigh ethical arguments.

As is evident from the descriptions above, if teachers use only traditional forms of assessment, they will be unable to assess many aspects (some would say the most important aspects) of student learning. Clearly, other methods such as constructed-response tests, projects, and behavior are needed. These alternative modes must therefore be designed and procedures developed for the evaluation of student work produced through these alternative means.

DESIGN ISSUES

Measurement experts argue that most aspects of student knowledge and skill may be assessed through well-designed multiple-choice tests. They point to well-known tests that evaluate problem-solving, reasoning, and data analysis. On further examination, by looking at the actual items, most teachers would probably agree that the items require some higher-level thinking on the part of students.

Teachers should not assume because such test items are possible to construct that they themselves can construct them, or should want to spend the necessary time to do so. These test items are designed by measurement experts and are extensively field-tested to ensure that they are both valid and reliable. Neither of these conditions is available to most practicing educators, who have their next day's lessons to think about.

When teachers try to design their own multiple-choice tests, they encounter three related, though somewhat distinct, difficulties:

• *Ambiguity.* A major challenge confronting test developers is to create multiple-choice test items in which the wrong answers are plausible and yet, are unambiguously wrong. Ideally, the distracters (the wrong answers) should be incorrect in ways in which students' thinking is typically flawed, so a student's pattern of wrong answers may reveal diagnostic information.

Such tests are very difficult to construct. Most teachers have had the experience of creating a test in which students can, by guessing or using a process of elimination, determine the right answer even when they know very little about the subject.

- *Authenticity.* In order to engage students in meaningful work, it is helpful for assessment to be as authentic as possible. Students are more likely to produce work of good quality if the questions seem plausible and worthwhile. But to design an authentic multiple-choice test, one that elicits the desired knowledge and skill, is very difficult. Highly authentic questions tend to be long and cumbersome, while more focused questions are often found to be boring and inauthentic by students.

- *Time.* Good multiple-choice questions require a great deal of time to create. And unless they are tested before being used, teachers cannot be sure that they are valid. That is, the question may be ambiguous, or several of the choices may be plausible. Hence, students are justified in challenging such questions and the evaluations based on them.

These factors, taken together, suggest that teachers are unlikely to be successful in creating their own multiple-choice tests for complex learning. Experts in test design can succeed more often than novices, but even experts are limited in what is possible through the technique.

INFLUENCE ON INSTRUCTION

Probably the most serious concern about the exclusive use of traditional testing relates to its effect on the instructional process. Since traditional tests are best suited to the assessment of low-level knowledge, such instructional goals are heavily represented (to the virtual exclusion of other, more complex, learning goals) in such tests.

It is well known that "what you test is what you get." Through our assessment methods we convey to students what is important to learn. And when the tests we give reflect only factual or procedural knowledge, we signal to students that such knowledge is more important than their ability to reason, to solve problems, to work together collaboratively, or to write effectively. Since multiple-choice tests are best at evaluating students' command of factual knowledge, many students equate school learning with trivial pursuit, and never realize that their teachers value the expression of their own ideas, a creative approach to problems, or the design of an imaginative experiment.

The most powerful means teachers have at their disposal for shifting the culture of their classrooms to one of significant work is to change their assessment methodologies. While traditional tests will always have a value, combining their use with alternative means sends an important signal to students regarding what sort of learning is valued in school. If good ideas and imaginative projects count, students will begin to shift their conceptions of the meaning of school.

SUMMARY

Traditional forms of assessment carry many disadvantages, which, when such tests are used exclusively, undermine the best intentions of teachers. These tests can evaluate only a narrow band of student learning and, even within that band, are extremely difficult to construct well.

THE BENEFITS OF PERFORMANCE ASSESSMENT

Many of the advantages of performance assessment are simply the reverse side of the limitations of traditional testing, namely, that they enable teachers to assess students in all those aspects of learning they value, in particular, writing and speaking, reasoning and problem solving, psychomotor and social skills, and the entire affective domain. However, there are many other benefits to be derived as well. These are described below.

CLARITY AS TO CRITERIA AND STANDARDS

When teachers use performance assessment, they discover that they must be extremely clear, both to themselves and to their students, as to the criteria they will use to evaluate student work, and the standard of performance they expect. For many teachers, this clarity is greater than that required for traditional testing, and requires that they give sustained thought to difficult questions such as "What do I really want my students to be able to do?" and "What is most important in this unit?" and "How good is good enough?"

These questions, while some of the most important that teachers ever consider, tend to be obscured by the pressure of daily work, and the normal routines of life in schools. The design of performance assessment tasks puts them at the center. Most teachers find that, while the questions are difficult to answer, their entire instructional program is greatly strengthened as a result of the effort.

PROFESSIONAL DIALOGUE ABOUT CRITERIA AND STANDARDS

If teachers create their performance assessments together, they must decide together how they will evaluate student work and what their standards will be. These are not easy discussions, but most teachers find them to be extremely valuable.

Occasionally, teachers find that their criteria for problem solving, for example, are very different from one another. One teacher may believe that the process used is more important than whether or not the answer is correct. Another may believe the reverse. They must resolve their differences in designing a problem-solving task, if they are to evaluate student work together. On the other hand, they could agree to disagree, and each use his or her own procedure. But the conversation will have been valuable in isolating such a fundamental difference in approach.

IMPROVED STUDENT WORK

Virtually all teachers report improved quality of student work when they begin using performance assessment. This is due, no doubt, to several factors:

- *Clarity as to criteria and standards.* Just as greater clarity as to criteria and standards is valuable to teachers and contributes to professional dialogue, it is essential for students. When students know what is expected, they are far more likely to be able to produce it than if they do not.

- *Greater confidence in work.* When students understand the criteria and standards to be used in evaluating their work, they can approach it with greater confidence. The criteria provide them with guidelines for their work and they can estimate the time required to produce work of good quality. All this tends to increase student engagement and pride in their work.

- *High expectations.* When they make the standards for exemplary performance clear to students, teachers are sending an important signal about their expectations. They are saying to students, in effect, "Here is how I define excellence. Anyone here can produce work of such quality by applying sufficient effort." This is a powerful message for students; it brings excellence within their reach.

- *Greater student engagement.* When students are involved in performance tasks, particularly those that are highly authentic, they are more likely to be highly motivated in their work than if they are answering trivial pursuit-type questions. As a consequence of this engagement, the quality of student work is generally high.

IMPROVED COMMUNICATION WITH PARENTS

Student work produced as part of a performance assessment is extremely meaningful to parents. If collected in a portfolio and used for parent conferences, these products can serve to document student learning (or its lack). If necessary, a student's work may be shown to parents next to that of another (anonymous) student, to illustrate differences in performance. Such documentation may be very helpful to teachers in persuading a parent of the need for additional educational services.

If student work as part of performance assessment is maintained in a portfolio, however, the selections should be made with care. There are many possible uses of a portfolio, and students can benefit from the reflection that accompanies their own selection of 'best work' entries. But as a documentation of student progress, items should be chosen that reflect student performance in all the important instructional goals. For example, if a math program consists of eight strands taught through 12 units, the selections made should document each of the units, and all the strands. These issues will be discussed more fully in Chapter 3 (Making an Evaluation Plan).

A WORD ABOUT GRADING

Many educators ask about converting the results of performance assessment to traditional grades. There are no easy answers to this question for the simple reason that the issue of grading does not lend itself to simplistic approaches. The reasons for this difficulty, however, are not related to performance assessment, but to the varied methods and purposes for assigning grades.

A "score" on a performance assessment is a straightforward matter; student work is evaluated against a clear standard and a judgment made as to where it stands against that standard. If students' grades are also intended (solely) to reflect the degree of mastery of the curriculum, then the score on the performance assessment can be translated in a fairly linear way to a grade. A score of "4" could be an "A," a "3" could be a "B" and so forth.

However, there are several reasons why such a procedure may not be ideal. For one thing, most teachers use other methods in addition to performance tasks to assess student learning. The typical evaluation plan used by a teacher will include tests as well as performance items. Therefore, the results from different methods must be combined in some manner, including weighting some items more than others.

In addition, many teachers incorporate other elements in addition to achievement against a standard into a grade. They may want to build in the degree of progress from earlier work, for example, or the amount of effort or discipline displayed by a student. Alternatively, teachers may have offered some students a lot of coaching in their performance assessments (thereby using them also as teaching tools) and they may recognize that the students' performance reflects more than what they could do on their own.

Therefore, while performance assessments may not translate directly into grades, it may be a good idea to establish some connection between them, making the necessary provision for combining scores on different assessments. If this is done, it sends powerful messages to students. Primarily, such a procedure takes the mystery out of grading, and allows students to know in advance the criteria by which their work will be evaluated. In addition, it also conveys to students that high grades are within the reach of all students. Over time they recognize that if they work hard, they (all of them) can do well. In this situation, good grades are not rationed; all students whose work is at the highest standard can get an "A." As students come to internalize this awareness, and act upon it, it can transform a classroom into a far more purposeful place, and one in which students are concerned with the quality of their work.

SUMMARY

The use of performance assessment conributes many important benefits, beyond strictly measurement issues, to the culture of a classroom. These advantages are derived from clarity of criteria and standards, and benefit teachers, students, and parents.

3

MAKING AN EVALUATION PLAN

Designing and implementing performance assessment entails a major investment of time and energy. In order to ensure that this investment is a wise one, and yields the desired benefits, it is essential to work from a plan. How to develop such a plan, and coordinate it with a school or district's curriculum, is the subject of this chapter.

A CURRICULUM MAP

A useful approach to developing an assessment plan for mathematics instruction is to begin with a consideration of goals in the mathematics curriculum as a whole. An assessment plan, after all, should have as its goal the assessment of student learning in the curriculum; it makes no sense in isolation from that curriculum. Therefore, a plan for assessment should be created with the whole curriculum in mind.

MAJOR OUTCOMES, GOALS, OR STRANDS

A good place to start in thinking about the assessment demands of the curriculum is to consider the curriculum's major outcomes, goals, or strands. Most listings of major mathematics outcomes, or listings of mathematics goals by strand are organized, at least loosely, around the standards published by the National Council of Teachers of Mathematics (NCTM) in 1989. These standards have had an enormous and positive influence on the teaching of mathematics, and have caused educators everywhere to think more deeply about what they teach and how to engage their students in conceptual understanding. The NCTM standards are organized in 13 major areas:

- mathematics as problem solving
- mathematics as communication
- mathematics as reasoning
- mathematical connections
- numbers and number relationships
- number systems and number theory
- computation and estimation
- patterns and functions
- algebra
- statistics
- probability
- geometry
- measurement

Most schools and districts now use some variation on the NCTM standards to organize their mathematics curriculum into major strands, or around major outcomes. Naturally, the numbers and number relationships, for example, taught in the second grade are very different from those in eighth grade but the concept is addressed at both levels. The strands provide the unifying themes that are carried through the entire mathematics program.

Some states, through the State Department of Education, have mandated (or highly recommended) mathematics goals or outcomes also derived from the NCTM standards. For example, Pennsylvania has identified seven major mathematics outcomes. These are, briefly:

- numbers and number systems
- estimation, computation, and measurement with the appropriate use of technology
- patterns, functions, and relations
- formulating and solving problems and communicating the results

- algebra and geometry
- charts, tables and graphs
- statistics and probability

Other states, for example California, have also identified major mathematics outcomes, or strands. Local districts then base their broad goals for mathematics education on those they receive from their state. For example, the Norfolk, Virginia, public schools specify the following:

- computation
- estimation
- organizing data
- analyzing problems
- formulating conclusions
- determining logical solutions

These broad goals, outcomes, or strands provide the framework for curriculum planning. They do not comprise a curriculum; that is developed from the outcomes for each grade level. But they do offer guidance for those preparing the curriculum at each stage.

TOPICS OR UNITS

What students work on every day, and the way in which most mathematics textbooks are organized, is a series of topics or units, rather than outcomes or strands. For example, in a typical seventh grade mathematics text, the chapters concern:

- addition and subtraction expressions
- multiplication and division expressions
- multiplication and division of decimals
- graphing and statistics
- geometry and measurement
- addition and subtraction of fractions
- multiplication and division of fractions
- integers and rational numbers
- ratio, proportion, and percent
- geometry

- area and volume
- algebra and coordinate geometry
- probability

Clearly, some of the topics fit well with some of the strands. For example, the concepts taught in the "geometry" chapter would address the goals in the "geometry" strand. But some of the other connections are not nearly so obvious. In which chapter, for instance, would one find material related to "mathematics as communication," or "estimation?" If educators are committed to addressing all the goals stated or implied in the NCTM *Standards*, or the equivalent document from their own state or district, then they must match the topics or units they teach with the goals inherent in those standards. The best technique to use for this purpose is a matrix, which is described in the next section. A sample matrix is presented on the next page. (Figure 3.1)

CREATING THE CURRICULUM MAP

Across the top of the matrix are listed all the strands, major goals, or outcomes of the mathematics program. In the matrix provided, the ones listed are those developed by the New Standards Project. Down the left-hand side are listed all the topics or units in the year's curriculum, organized, insofar as can be known, in sequence. Then, for each unit or topic, teachers should consider which of the strands or outcomes the topic addresses, and place an X in the corresponding box.

In some cases, research is needed in order to know where to place the X's. For example, if one of the major strands is estimation, many topics may be used to develop that skill, but some are probably better than others; estimation is probably better suited as a component of computation than of geometry. Furthermore, some textbooks will develop the skill of estimation in the context of one topic, others in another. It may be an empirical question then, which topics may be used to develop which of the outcomes, and can be determined by examining the text in use.

What results from this process is a map of the curriculum,

FIGURE 3.1 CURRICULUM/ASSESSMENT PLANNING GUIDE
MATHEMATICS

Course/Grade _____

Outcomes / Units or Topics	Numbers and Number Systems	Computation Measurement Estimation & Technology	Patterns Functions Relations	Formulate & Solve Problems; Communicate	Algebra Geometry Probability Statistics	Charts Tables Graphs	Statistics Probability

demonstrating the ways in which the different strands or outcomes are (or can be, given the textbook in use) addressed in each of the topics of the curriculum. No doubt some strands receive heavier emphasis than others. In most texts, for example, "computation" is much more heavily weighed than "patterns and functions."

If the map reveals large gaps in the curriculum, for example, if the curriculum map shows that some of the outcomes are not adequately addressed by the program in use, then some adjustments must be made. It is possible that a given curriculum lacks focus on an entire strand of the NCTM standards e.g., mathematical communication. In that case, educators will have to determine in which topics they could develop that skill. Once determined, they can then add X's to the appropriate boxes. For instance, they could decide to add, to each of their units, an objective and the corresponding instructional activities addressing the issue of student communication of the ideas of the unit, whether it is addition of fractions or measurement. In that way, they would adequately address all the different standards.

SUMMARY

A curriculum map can be used to define which units or topics in a curriculum may be used to help students acquire the knowledge and skills inherent in a state's mathematics framework. The map is created by local educators, using the appropriate framework and their own textbook, through the exercise of professional judgment.

ASSESSMENT METHODOLOGIES

Once the curriculum map has been produced, educators must determine how each of the outcomes and each of the topics are to be assessed. Some will lend themselves to traditional testing while others will require more complex performance assessment.

THE ROLE OF TRADITIONAL TESTING

Many mathematics curriculum goals may be assessed through traditional testing. It is, and will always be, important for students to be able to perform accurate computations, or to solve simple equations. The correct use of algorithms is an important part of mathematical literacy. For all these reasons, educators would be ill-advised to abandon the use of traditional tests as part of their total assessment plan.

However, traditional testing is limited in what it can achieve. As teachers survey the curriculum map they have produced, they discover that some of the X's they have written simply do not lend themselves to a multiple-choice or short-answer test. What kind of test, for example, could one construct that would assess students on their understanding of place value, or the use of patterns to solve a problem in number theory?

Moreover, many educators argue that the use of traditional tests, even in those areas of the curriculum where they would appear to be best suited, can do actual harm. This relates to the fact that some students, and their teachers, confuse procedural knowledge with conceptual understanding. That is, students learn a procedure, an algorithm, for getting "the right answer" with little or no understanding of how or why the procedure works, where it would be useful, or what the algorithm accomplishes. Therefore, they can take a test and solve problems correctly, with poor conceptual understanding. If the assessment procedures used do not reveal that lack of understanding, the students may move along to more complex concepts, ones that build on the previous ones, with an increasingly shaky foundation.

Therefore, while traditional tests may be highly useful in assessing certain aspects of the mathematics curriculum, they should be used with caution, and with full awareness of their limitations.

THE PLACE FOR PERFORMANCE ASSESSMENT

Performance assessment is the technique of choice for evaluating student understanding of much of the mathematics curriculum. When students are asked to complete a task, or when they are asked to explain their thinking, they reveal their understanding of complex topics.

Sometimes performance assessment in mathematics can consist of a small addition to traditional testing. For example, students might be asked to solve a fairly traditional problem, but then be asked to explain why they selected the approach they did. Their explanation will reveal their understanding of the process, or their lack of it, and will also serve to assess their skill in the communication of mathematical ideas.

In addition, the authentic application of mathematical procedures is highly motivational to students. Many students regard the applications problems (word problems) they encounter in most mathematics textbooks with disbelief; their reaction is frequently one of 'who cares?' However, with some thought, most teachers are able to create situations that students in their classes might actually encounter, which require the application of the mathematical ideas included in a given unit. The creation of such a task is the subject of Chapter 5, while the adaptation of an existing task is considered in Chapter 7.

A PLAN TO GET STARTED

The idea of creating (or even adapting) performance tasks for all those areas of the mathematics curriculum for which they would be well suited can be a daunting one. After all, if students as well as teachers are unfamiliar with such an approach it is likely to require more time than planned. And since it is unfamiliar, everyone involved is likely to encounter unexpected difficulties. How, then, should one begin?

In general, one should start small. When just beginning, most teachers find that they can use performance tasks only infrequently, at a rate of 4-6 per year. Such a schedule permits teachers the time to create or adapt their tasks to ensure that they will accomplish their desired purposes, and to evaluate student work carefully. But if only one or two tasks per quarter are administered, then they should be those that have the promise to reveal the maximum information about student understanding.

Once the techniques and practices of performance assessment are well understood, and once teachers and students both have some experience in the methodology, performance tasks may be used frequently. However, even with experience, few teachers will administer more than two or three such tasks per month.

SUMMARY

Based on the curriculum map, educators can create an evaluation plan. This plan will include both traditional testing and performance assessment. As they move to performance assessment, teachers are advised to start small.

4

EVALUATING COMPLEX PERFORMANCE

The major advantage of multiple-choice, matching and true/false tests concerns the ease of scoring them; it does not take long to mark an answer "right" or "wrong." Indeed, this speed and ease of correction is their primary value in large-scale testing programs. Because standardized tests are machine-scorable and consequently, inexpensive to administer, they can provide large amounts of data cheaply to school districts and states.

A student's performance on a multiple-choice or short-answer test may be described in terms of percentages. One student might score 87%, another 94%, still another 68%. But when teachers use other assessment methodologies, the concept of "percent correct" loses much of its meaning. What is 87% of an essay? How good (and in what way) should a skit be to receive a score of 94%?

These are not simple questions, and their answers constitute the heart of performance assessment. But there are answers, and answers that respect the important measurement principles of equity, validity, and reliability. This section, through a non-school example, introduces the techniques of evaluating performance, and then discusses each of the issues raised.

A NON-SCHOOL EXAMPLE

All the principles involved in the evaluation of complex performance may be illustrated by an everyday example: that of going to a restaurant. By reading through this example, readers will address, in a familiar form, all the issues they will encounter in designing systems of performance assessment for classroom use. Moreover, it will be evident that the methods for evaluating performance reflect, at their heart, only common sense.

THE SITUATION

Let's imagine that we are opening a restaurant in your town, and that we are at the point of hiring waiters and waitresses. We know that it is important that the waiters and waitresses be skilled, so we want to hire the best we can find. As part of our search, we have decided to eat in some restaurants already in existence, to see if there are people working in these establishments that we can lure away to our restaurant. Consequently, we are preparing to embark on our search mission.

THE CRITERIA

How will we know what to look for? We must determine the five or six most important qualities we would watch for in a good waiter or waitress. But since our focus here is on "performance," we should list only those qualities that are visible to a customer (such as appearance), and not other qualities which, while they might be important to an employer (such as getting to work on time) are not seen by a customer.

A reasonable list of criteria will include such qualities as: Courtesy, Appearance, Responsiveness, Knowledge, Coordination, Accuracy. It is important to write the criteria using neutral, rather than positive, words. That is, for reasons that will soon become apparent, we should write "appearance" rather than "neat."

These criteria could become, of course, a checklist. That is, we could eat in a restaurant and determine whether our server was courteous, responsive, or knowledgeable, etc. We could answer each of the items with a "yes" or "no," and then count the "yeses." However, life tends to be more complicated than a checklist. That is, a waiter or waitresss is somewhat knowledgeable, mostly accurate, a little bit coordinated.

How do we accommodate these degrees of performance? How can we design a system that respects the complexity of the performance, and which we can use to actually compare two or more individuals? The answer is to create a "rubric," a scoring guide.

THE SCORING GUIDE OR RUBRIC

A rubric is simply a guide for evaluating performance, and is presented below.

FIGURE 4.1 WAITER/WAITRESS RUBRIC

	Level One	Level Two	Level Three	Level Four
Courtesy				
Appearance				
Responsiveness				
Knowledge				
Coordination				
Accuracy				

In the left column are listed the different criteria we have determined are important for waiters and waitresses in our fledgling restaurant. Across the top are four columns for different levels of performance. In this case, there are four levels, and the double line between levels two and three indicates that performance at levels three and four is acceptable, and performance at levels one and two is unacceptable. We could, then, broadly define the different levels as:

Level One: "Very poor," or "Terrible" or "Completely unacceptable"
Level Two: "Not quite good enough," or "Almost"
Level Three: "Acceptable," or "Good enough but not great"
Level Four: "Wonderful," "Exemplary," or "Terrific"

In each box, then, we would write descriptions of actual performance that would represent each level for each criterion. For example, for "coordination" we might decide that an individual at level one actually spilled an entire bowl of soup, or a cup of coffee, or could not handle a tray of dishes; someone at level two spilled a little coffee in the saucer, or let some water spill while filling the glasses; a waiter at level three spilled nothing, and someone at level four balanced many items without mishap.

We could fill in the entire chart with such descriptions, and we would then be ready to go evaluate prospective employees. A possible profile might look like the following:

FIGURE 4.2 COMPLETED WAITER/WAITRESS RUBRIC

Name   Wendy Jones   Restaurant   Hilltop Cafe

	Level One	Level Two	Level Three	Level Four
Courtesy		X		
Appearance				X
Responsiveness			X	
Knowledge	X			
Coordination				X
Accuracy			X	

We would still have to decide, of course, whether to hire this individual. Or whether this individual was preferable to another candidate whose scores were all '3's.' That is, we would have to determine how to arrive at a composite score for each individual, so we could compare them.

Naturally, if we were using this approach not for hiring, but for supervision, we would not need to combine scores on the different criteria; we could use them simply for feedback and coaching. For example, since this individual is, apparently, not very knowledgeable, we could provide assistance in that area. We could then work on courtesy, and make sure that customers feel comfortable around this person. That is, for supervision purposes, the system is diagnostic, and enables us, as owners of the restaurant, to provide specific and substantive feedback on areas needing improvement.

SUMMARY

Creating a scoring rubric for a non-school activity provides an illustration of the principles involved in performance assessment.

MEASUREMENT AND PRACTICAL ISSUES

When we contemplate applying these principles to the evaluation of student performance, we encounter a number of issues which, while not technically complex, must be addressed before this approach can be implemented. It should be borne in mind, however, that most teachers have rubrics in their minds for student performance; they apply these every time they grade a student's paper. However, communication is vastly improved if educators can be explicit about the criteria they use in evaluating student work, and what their expectations are. This need for clarity requires us to address a number of technical and practical issues, which are described below.

THE NUMBER AND TYPE OF CRITERIA

For a given performance, how many criteria should we have? For example, when evaluating a persuasive essay, how many different things should we look for? Should we evaluate organization separately from structure? What about the use of language? Or specifically, the use of vocabulary? Or correct spelling and mechanics? What about sentence structure and organization? Should we consider the essay's impact on us, the reader? Is it important that we are actually persuaded by the argument?

Clearly, some of these elements are related to one another; it would be difficult, in a persuasive essay, to have good use of language independently of the vocabulary used. However, other criteria are completely separate from one another. Unless it is so poor as to hinder communication, a student's inadequacies in mechanics and spelling will not affect the persuasiveness of the argument.

The number of criteria used should reflect, insofar as it is possible to predict, those aspects of performance which are simultaneously important and are independent of one another. They will also reflect the age and skill of the students. For example, with young children or special education students it might be necessary to identify specific aspects of punctuation that are evaluated, i.e., proper use of capital letters, commas, and semi-colons; whereas for high school students these may all be clustered under "punctuation" and can include all aspects of mechanics.

However, when criteria are clustered in such a way that they include several elements, these should be specifically identified. Just as, in the waiter and waitress example, "appearance" might include the person's uniform, condition of the hair and nails, and general grooming, individual criteria should specify what elements are included. For example, "use of language" might include richness of vocabulary, use of persuasive words, and proper use of specialized terms.

The criteria, moreover, should reflect those aspects of performance which are truly most important, not merely those which are easiest to see or count. Thus, a rubric for writing should include more than spelling and mechanics; a rubric for problem-solving should include criteria dealing with the student's thought processes and methods of approach.

A rubric should not include so many criteria that it is difficult to use. On the other hand, it should include every important element. As a general rule, since most people cannot hold more than five or six items in their mind simultaneously, rubrics should not contain more than five or six criteria.

ANALYTIC VS. HOLISTIC RUBRICS

The waiter/waitress rubric developed in the previous section is an example of an *analytic* rubric, that is, different criteria are identified and levels of performance are described for each. Using such a rubric in the classroom, in which different criteria are defined and described, makes it possible to analyze student work as to its strengths and weaknesses.

With a *holistic* rubric, on the other hand, the features of performance on all criteria for a given score are combined, so it is possible, for example, to describe a "level two" waiter, or a "level four" waitress. Such holistic judgments are necessary when a single score, such as on an Advanced Placement test, must be given. However, compromises are always necessary, since an individual piece of work will usually not include all the features of a certain level. Therefore, analytic rubrics are recommended for classroom use, since they provide much more complete information to be used for feedback to students.

However, even for classroom use, when rubrics are used to evaluate student work, they may be applied either analytically or holistically. That is, student performance may be evaluated on each element of the rubric, and feedback provided on each. Alternatively, a teacher can examine a piece of student work as a whole, and apply a rubric more holistically. Which approach is used will depend on the amount, and level of detail, of feedback desired. For the samples of student work included in this book, the rubrics are written analytically, but they are applied holistically. This permits careful analysis of each student work sample, yet an efficient summary of the salient features of each.

HOW MANY POINTS ON THE SCALE?

In the waiter/waitress example, we identified four points

on the scale. That was an arbitrary decision; we could have selected more, or fewer. Performance on any criterion, after all, falls along a continuum; designating points on a scale represents, to some degree, a compromise between practical demands and the complexity of real performance. However, in deciding on the number of points to use, there are two important considerations to bear in mind:

- *Fineness of distinctions.* More points offer the opportunity to make very fine distinctions between levels of performance. However, scales with many points are time-consuming to use, since the differences between different points are likely to be small.

- *Even vs. odd.* In general an even number of points is preferable to an odd number. This relates to the measurement principle of "central tendency," which states that many people, if given the opportunity, will assign a score in the middle of a range. If there is no middle, as on a scale with an even number of points, they are required to make a commitment to one side or the other.

However, these considerations apply to rubrics that are constructed to apply to a single activity or type of performance. For developmental rubrics, a large number of points may be preferable. In a developmental rubric, students' performance over an extended period of time is monitored on a single rubric. Used most commonly in Foreign Language classes, such a rubric might define oral language proficiency from the most rudimentary through the level displayed by a native speaker. Every student of the language will perform somewhere, at all times, on that rubric, which might have, perhaps 10 points. A second-year student might be functioning at, say, level "3," while a fourth-year student might be at level "5." Both would have made good progress, and yet would have a distance to go before performing at the level of a native speaker. For such purposes, a developmental rubric with many points on the scale is extremely useful, since it can be used to chart progress over many years.

DIVIDING LINE BETWEEN ACCEPTABLE AND
UNACCEPTABLE PERFORMANCE

It is important to decide at the outset where the line will be between acceptable and unacceptable performance. This activity is at the heart of setting a standard, since teachers thereby communicate to their colleagues as well as their students, the quality of work they expect.

In the waiter/waitress example, the line between acceptable and unacceptable performance was established between levels "2" and "3." This, too, is arbitrary; it could just as well been put between the "1" and the "2." When determining where to place the dividing line, educators should consider several points:

- *Use.* If a scoring rubric is to be used for formative evaluation, it is helpful to identify several levels of "unacceptable," since, in that way, teachers can know quickly whether a student's performance on a certain criterion is close to being acceptable or far away. Such knowledge can guide further instruction. On the other hand, if a rubric is to be used to make a summative judgment only, then it is less important if a student's performance is close to the cut-off point; in this case, unacceptable is unacceptable, without regard to degrees of unacceptability.

- *Number of points on the scale.* If a scoring rubric is constructed with six, seven, or eight points, then the placement of the "unacceptable" line might be different from a rubric with only four points. A five-point scale (while not ideal from the standpoint of having an odd number of points) enables two levels of unacceptable while also permitting finer degrees of excellence, with the upper levels representing "barely acceptable," "good," and "excellent."

- *Developmental vs. performance-specific rubrics.* Clearly, for a developmental rubric, one that defines performance over an extended period of time, there is no need to define the distinction between "acceptable" and "unacceptable" performance in the same manner as for a performance-specific rubric. That is, it may be reasonable for a second-year language student to perform at level "3" on a ten-point scale, whereas such performance would not be good enough for a fourth-year student. In this case, judgments as to acceptability and expectations do not reside in the rubric, but in the use that is made of them in different settings.

TITLES FOR LEVELS OF PERFORMANCE

Closely related to the need to define the cut-off between acceptable and unacceptable performance is the requirement to broadly define the labels for each point on the rubric. For professional use, teachers often use terms like "unacceptable," and "exemplary." Such titles might work even if students (or their parents) will see the rubric, but it should be given some thought. Some educators prefer names like "novice," "emerging," "proficient," and "distinguished." Decisions as to the best headings are matters for professional judgment and consensus.

DESCRIPTIONS OF PERFORMANCE

Descriptions for levels of performance should be written in language that is truly descriptive, rather than comparative. For example, words such as "average" should be avoided, as in "the number of computational errors is average," and replaced by statements such as "the solution contains only minor computational errors." "Minor" will then have to be defined, for example, as an error not resulting in an erroneous conclusion, or an error that was clearly based in carelessness.

GENERIC VS. TASK-SPECIFIC

Constructing a performance rubric for student work takes considerable time, particularly if it is a joint effort among many educators. The issues of time and the desirability of sending a consistent signal to students and their parents regarding standards, are important reasons to try to create generic rubrics.

Such rubrics may be used for many different specific tasks that students do.

The areas of student performance that appear to lend themselves best to generic rubrics are such things as lab reports, problem-solving, expository, descriptive or persuasive essays, group projects, and oral presentations. Some of these, such as oral presentations, may even be suitable for several different disciplines. It is highly valuable for students to know that when they are preparing an oral presentation, it will always be evaluated, in every setting, using the same criteria.

However, generic rubrics however, are not always possible or even desirable. The elements of problem-solving, and certainly the levels of acceptable performance are very different for high school sophomores than those for second graders. Similarly, the specific elements of a lab report change as students become more sophisticated and more knowledgeable. So while there are many reasons to construct rubrics as generic as possible — and intra- and cross-departmental discussions are highly recommended — it may not be possible to completely develop generic rubrics, even for those aspects of performance in which students are engaged over a period of many years. There are many tasks, and many types of tasks, which require their own task-specific rubrics.

PROFESSIONAL CONSENSUS

When teachers work together to determine descriptions of levels of performance in a scoring rubric, they may find that they do not completely agree. This is natural and to be expected. After all, it is well documented that teachers grade student work quite differently from one another.

Discussions as to the proper wording of different levels of performance constitute rich professional dialogue. While difficult, the discussions are generally enriching for everyone involved; most teachers find that their ideas can be enhanced by the contributions of their colleagues. Rubrics that are the product of many minds are generally superior to those created by individuals. In addition, if a number of teachers find that they can use the same, or similar, rubrics for evaluating student work, communication with students is that much more consistent, resulting in better quality work.

INTER-RATER AGREEMENT

Closely related to consensus on the wording of descriptions of levels of performance is the matter of agreement on the application of the rubric. The only way to be sure that different individuals agree on the meaning of the descriptions of different levels is to actually apply the statements to samples of student work.

The importance of this issue cannot be exaggerated. It is a fundamental principle of equity and fairness that evaluation of a student's work be the same regardless of who is doing the evaluating. However, teachers very rarely agree completely at the beginning. Occasionally, two teachers will evaluate a single piece of student work very differently, even when they have agreed on the scoring rubric. In those cases, they generally discover that they were interpreting words in the rubric very differently, or that the words used were themselves ambiguous. Only trying the rubric with actual student work will reveal such difficulties.

When preparing rubrics for evaluating student work, therefore, the project is not totally complete until examples of different levels of performance have been selected to illustrate the points on the scale. Called "anchor papers" these samples can serve to maintain consistency in scoring.

CLARITY OF DIRECTIONS

Another fundamental principle of fairness and equity concerns the directions given to students. Any criterion to be evaluated must be clearly asked for in the directions to a performance task. For example, if students are to be evaluated for their originality in making an oral presentation, something in the directions to them should recommend that they present it in an original or creative manner. Likewise, if students are to be evaluated for the organization of their data, they should know that organization is important. Otherwise, from a student's point of view, it is necessary to read the mind of the teacher and to guess what is important.

Some teachers find that they can engage students in the development of the rubric itself. Students, they discover, know the indicators of a good oral presentation or of a well-solved problem. While students' thoughts are rarely well enough organized to enable them to create a rubric on their own, their ideas make good additions to a rubric already drafted by the teacher.

There are many advantages to engaging students in the construction of a scoring rubric. Most obviously, they know what is included and can therefore focus their work. But even more important, students tend to do better work, with greater pride in it and greater attention to quality when the evaluation criteria are clear. Suddenly, school is not a matter of "gotcha," it is a place where excellent work is both defined and expected.

COMBINING SCORES ON CRITERIA

Occasionally, it is important to be able to combine scores on different criteria and to arrive at a single evaluation. For example, teachers must occasionally rank students, or convert their judgments on performance to a grade or to a percentage. How can this be done? In arriving at a single, holistic score, several issues must be addressed:

- *Weight.* Are all the criteria of equal importance? Unless one or another is designated as more or less important than the others, they should all be assumed to be of equal importance. Educators should have good reasons for their decisions as to weight, and these discussions can themselves constitute important professional conversations. As an example, we could have determined, in our creation of the rubric for a waiter or waitress, that "knowledge" is the most important criterion and is worth twice the value of the others. Then, our rubric and the points possible from each point, appear on the following page:

- *Calculations.* How should the scores be calculated?

FIGURE 4.3 WAITER/WAITRESS RUBRIC

Name   Wendy Jones   Restaurant   Hilltop Cafe

	Level One	Level Two	Level Three	Level Four
Courtesy Weight = 1		X		
Appearance Weight = 1				X
Responsiveness Weight = 1			X	
Knowledge Weight = 2	X			
Coordination Weight = 1				X
Accuracy Weight = 1			X	

Scores: (score assigned) x (weight) = (criterion score)
     criterion score on each criterion = total score
     total score / total possible scores = percentage score

Using this procedure for Wendy Jones, her point score would be as follows:

Courtesy:	2 (2 x 1)
Appearance:	4 (4 x 1)
Responsiveness:	3 (3 x 1)
Knowledge:	2 (1 x 2)
Coordination:	4 (4 x 1)
Accuracy:	3 (3 x 1)
Total:	18

On this rubric, the total possible points for each criterion are:

Courtesy:	4
Appearance:	4
Responsiveness:	4
Knowledge:	8
Responsiveness:	4
Accuracy:	4
Total points:	28

Therefore, to calculate a total score, we convert the points received to a percentage of the total possible points. Both the points received and the number of possible points reflect the weights assigned to each criterion. Thus, in our example, Wendy Jones would have received a score of 18, which, when divided by 28 is 64%.

- *Cut score.* What is the overall level of acceptable performance? We have, of course, defined the line between acceptable and unacceptable performance for each criterion earlier. However, now we must determine a score which, overall, represents acceptable performance. We could set it as a percentage, for example 70%, in which case Wendy Jones would not be hired in our restaurant. Alternatively, we could establish a rule that no more than one criterion may be rated at a score below "3." This decision, like all the others made in constructing a performance rubric, is a matter of professional judgment.

TIME

Both for large-scale assessment and in the classroom, teachers know that multiple choice, short-answer, matching, and true/false tests take far less time to score than essay or open-ended tests. It is a relatively simple matter to take a stack of student tests and grade them against an answer key. Many educators fear that using performance tasks and rubrics will consume more time than they have or want to devote to it.

There is some validity to this concern. It is true that the evaluation of student work, using a rubric, takes more time than does grading student tests against a key. Also, the rubric itself can take considerable time to create.

However, there are two important issues to consider, one related to the increasing ease of using performance tasks, and the second related to the benefits derived from their use.

- *Decreasing time demands.* When they are just beginning to use performance tasks and rubrics, many teachers find that the time requirements are far greater than those needed for traditional tests. However, as they become more skilled, and as the rubrics they have developed prove to be useful for other assignments or other types of work, they discover that they can evaluate student work very efficiently, and in many cases in less time than the time required for traditional tests.

- *Other benefits.* In any event, most teachers discover that the benefits derived from increased use of performance tasks and rubrics vastly outweigh the additional time needed. They discover that students produce better quality work, and that they take greater pride in that work. If used as a component in assigning grades, teachers find that they can justify their decisions far more reliably than before they were using rubrics.

"Subjectivity" vs. "Objectivity"

One of the most important reservations about the use of rubrics to evaluate student work concerns their perceived "subjectivity" compared to "objective" multiple-choice tests. Such fears, while understandable, are completely unjustified.

First, it is important to remember that the only objective feature to a multiple-choice test is its scoring; answers are unambiguously right or wrong. However, many professional judgments have entered into making the test, and even into determining which of the possible answers are the correct ones. Someone must decide what questions to ask and how to structure the problems. These decisions reflect a vision of what is important knowledge and skill for students to demonstrate, and are based on professional judgment.

Similarly, in the construction of a scoring rubric, many decisions must be made; these, too, are made on the basis of professional judgment. But the fact that they are made by teachers in their classrooms, rather than by testing companies, does not make them less valid judgmentally. In fact, it may be argued that, if well thought out, such judgments are superior to those made by anonymous agencies far from the realities of one's own classroom.

In any event, scoring rubrics to evaluate student work and standardized tests are both grounded in professional judgment; they are absolutely equivalent on that score. In both cases, it is the quality of the judgments that is important, and the classroom-based judgment may be as good as that made by the testing company.

SUMMARY

In using scoring rubrics to evaluate student work, many issues must be taken into consideration. However, these issues, such as the number of points on the scale, or the importance of inter-rater agreement, are primarily a matter of common sense.

5

CREATING A PERFORMANCE TASK

The evaluation plan which results from the analysis of curriculum outcomes and topics (determined in Chapter 3) provides the guidelines needed to actually design performance tasks. As part of that plan, educators will have decided which topics or units lend themselves to the corresponding outcome goals or strands, and will have determined the best evaluation strategy for each. This analysis provides the basis for developing specifications (or requirements) for each performance task.

It is important to remember that a performance task is not simply something fun to do with one's students; it is not merely an activity. While it may involve student activity, and it may be fun, it is highly purposeful. A performance task is designed to assess learning, and it must be designed with that fundamental purpose in mind. In the design of performance tasks, a number of factors must be taken into consideration. These are described in this chapter.

SIZE OF PERFORMANCE TASKS

Performance tasks may be large or small. Large tasks take on many of the characteristics of instructional units, and students tend to derive much benefit from them. Large tasks may require a week or more to complete. They are typically complex and authentic, and require students to synthesize information from many sources. Small tasks, on the other hand, are more like open-ended test questions in which students solve a problem and explain their reasoning. These may be completed in a single class period or less. Naturally, tasks may be of medium length and complexity.

In deciding whether to use performance tasks that are large or small, educators must take a number of factors into account. These are outlined below.

PURPOSE

Teachers should be very clear about their purpose in using the performance task. What do they hope and plan to derive from it? Are their purposes purely those of assessment, or do they hope to accomplish some instructional purposes as well?

- *Small tasks are primarily suitable for purely assessment purposes.* If a teacher has taught a concept, for example the distinction between area and perimeter, and simply wants to know that students have understood that concept, then a small performance task is desirable. Such a task will ask students to solve a relatively small problem, to explain their thinking, and to show their work. However, it will not, in itself, also contain activities to be completed as part of the task. The task itself is designed purely for assessment.

- *Large tasks carry instructional purposes as well as assessment ones.* Occasionally, a teacher will want students to truly learn new content as a result of completing an assessment task. If so, a larger task, spread over a number of days, involving many sub-activities, will accomplish this purpose better than a small task.

- *Large tasks are better suited to culminating assessments than are small ones.* If performance tasks are to be used as culminating assessments, they are better if they are quite large and tap a number of different types of skills. However, if performance tasks are for the purpose of assessing a small part of the curriculum, small tasks are more useful since they can be administered frequently and the results used for adjusting instruction. The purpose of the assessment will be a major factor, then, in determining whether performance tasks should be large or small.

CURRICULUM PRESSURE AND TIME DEMANDS

Generally speaking, when teachers are under pressure to "cover" many topics in the curriculum, and consequently have little time to spend on any one topic, they may find that small performance tasks are all that they have time for. Large tasks, while they include many benefits not derived from small ones, do require lots of time, frequently more than many teachers have to devote to them.

SKILL IN GETTING STARTED

Most educators, when they are just beginning to use performance tasks, are unsure of what they are doing; in such situations it is a good idea to use the "start small" principle. For example, when not sure whether the directions to students on a task are clear, it is better to discover that after the students have spent a class period, rather than a week, completing the task. Less time has been lost and there may well be an opportunity to attempt another version of the same task, or a different task, later.

SUMMARY

The size of a performance task is best determined by its purpose (immediate or culminating assessment, or instruction) and by the time constraints and experience of the teacher. In general, it is recommended that teachers begin their efforts with performance assessment using tasks which are small rather than large. This provides the opportunity to experiment with a new methodology in a way that carries low stakes for success, for both the students and the teacher.

CRITERIA FOR GOOD PERFORMANCE TASKS

There is no doubt that some performance tasks are better

than others. What makes the good ones good? How can teachers, in designing or selecting performance tasks ensure that they are as good as possible? Several important qualities of good performance tasks are described below.

Engaging

The most important single criterion of performance tasks is that they are engaging to students; it is essential that they be of interest and that students want to put forth their best effort. This suggests that the questions asked have intrinsic merit so that students don't read the question and respond "So what?" or "Who cares?"

How does one find or create engaging tasks? As with so much else in education, professional judgment is the key. Successful instructional activities can be a good place to begin; most teachers know which activities, or which types of activities, are successful with their students. One of these activities, when adapted to the demands of assessment, might make a good performance task. And when reviewing tasks that others have created, one important criterion to always bear in mind is whether the task is likely to be engaging to students.

Authentic

Related to engagement is the issue of authenticity. Students tend to be more interested in those situations that resemble "real life" rather than those which are completely divorced from any practical application. In addition, performance tasks that reflect the "messiness" of real life make demands on students that more sanitized situations do not. Other things being equal, it is preferable to design or adapt performance tasks that represent authentic applications of knowledge and skill. Such authenticity requires students to use their knowledge and skill in much the same way it is used by adult practitioners in that field. A "template" to be used for designing authentic tasks is provided as Figure 5.2 at the end of the chapter.

However, authenticity is not always possible. Some important school learning is purely abstract, or makes sense only within its own context. For example, when we want students to demonstrate that they can analyze a character in literature, we must ask them to do that, even though such a task has no exact equivalents in "real life." Furthermore, a student's skill in analyzing a literary character assesses not only how well the student understands the character, but the degree to which he or she understands the structure of the piece of literature of which the character is a part.

Similarly, much of mathematics is highly formal and abstract. And while teachers care that students can apply their mathematical knowledge to practical situations, there is much of mathematics, such as number theory, which is internal to the discipline. But such knowledge must be assessed, and a constructed-response question is preferable to a multiple-choice item. However, such a question will probably not reflect authentic application.

ELICITS DESIRED KNOWLEDGE AND SKILL

A good performance task must assess what we want it to assess. It must, in other words, be aligned to the instructional goals we are interested in. Furthermore, the task should be designed in such a way that a student can complete the task correctly only by using the knowledge and skills being assessed.

We should never underestimate our students in this regard. While most students are not devious, most try to complete a task with as little risk and/or effort as possible. If they see an easy way to do the task, even by short-circuiting our intentions, they may well do it that way. Teachers should attempt, therefore, to create tasks that are as tight as possible, without being unduly rigid.

ENABLES ASSESSMENT OF INDIVIDUALS

Many performance tasks that sound imaginative are designed to be completed by students working in groups. And while such tasks may be valuable instructional activities and are certainly fun for the students, they cannot be used for the assessment of individuals. Assessment, after all, concerns the evaluation of individual learning; a performance task in which the contributions of different individuals is obscured cannot be used for such evaluation.

It is possible, of course, to design a performance task that includes both group and individual elements. For example, a group of students may be given some data and asked to analyze it. However, if the analysis is done as a group, each student should be required to produce an independent summary of what the data shows, and each individual's paper should be evaluated independently.

However, even in such a situation, the information for the teacher is somewhat compromised. When reading the work of an individual, a teacher knows only what that student could produce after having participated in a group with other students. With a different group of peers, that same student might have demonstrated much greater, or far less, understanding.

In general, then, it is preferable to create individual performance tasks if these are to be used solely for assessment purposes. If the goal also includes instructional purposes, then compromises on the individuality of the assessment tasks may be necessary.

CONTAINS CLEAR DIRECTIONS FOR STUDENTS

Any good performance task includes directions for students that are both complete and unambiguous. This is a fundamental principle of equity and good measurement. Students should never be in doubt about what it is they are to do on a performance task; the directions should be clear and complete. That does not mean that the directions should be lengthy; on the contrary, shorter directions are preferable to longer ones.

Secondly, the directions should specifically ask students to do everything on which they will be evaluated. For example, if one of the assessment criteria for a mathematics problem involves the organization of information, students should be specifically instructed to "present their information in an organized manner," or some such wording.

Related to the question of directions is that of scaffolding, that is, how much support should students receive in accomplishing the performance task? For example, in a mathematics problem that involves a multi-step solution, should the students be prompted for each step, or is that part of the problem? The answer to this question relates to the purposes of the assessment, and the age and skill level of the students. Less scaffolding is more authentic than more scaffolding; most problems are not presented to us with an outline of how to solve them. In general it is preferable to provide students with problems, with no scaffolding, that represent the optimal challenge for them to determine the proper approach on their own. An intermediate position is to present the problem, with no scaffolding, and then offer "tips" to the student to consider if desired. These tips can contain suggestions that, if followed, would provide guidance as to a possible approach to the problem.

SUMMARY

Good performance tasks share a number of important criteria. These should be borne in mind as tasks are designed.

THE DESIGN PROCESS

Now that the criteria for a performance task are clearly in mind, it is time to create one. What process should be followed? While there are several possible approaches, an effective one is described below.

CREATE AN INITIAL DESIGN

With the specifications and criteria in mind, create an initial draft of a performance task to assess a given combination of student understanding and skill. This task may be created using the format provided as Figure 5.1 at the end of the chapter, and it may, if authenticity is desired, follow the "template" offered in Figure 5.2. This initial draft should be considered as just that, an initial draft; it will almost certainly be revised later in the process.

OBTAIN COLLEAGUE REVIEW

If possible, persuade one or more colleagues to review your work. These may be teachers who work in the same discipline as you or with the same age students, or they may be teachers with very different responsibilities. Both approaches have their advantages and their drawbacks.

Teachers with different responsibilities are more likely to catch ambiguity or lack of clarity in the directions to students than are teachers who are as expert in the field as you are. On the other hand, expert colleagues are better able to spot situations in which the task is not completely valid, that is, situations in which students would be able to complete the task successfully without the desired knowledge and skill. Therefore, a colleague review that includes a combination of content experts and non-experts is ideal.

PILOT TASK WITH STUDENTS

Not until a performance task is tried with students is it possible to know whether it can accomplish its desired purpose. Only then can teachers know whether the directions are clear, whether all elements are properly requested, and whether the task truly elicits the desired knowledge and skill. Piloting with students is also the only way to know the degree to which the task is engaging to students.

Students are likely to be extremely honest in their reaction to a performance task. While it is possible to collect their feedback formally, it is generally evident, from their level of engagement and the quality of their responses, whether the task is a good one or not.

REVISE PERFORMANCE TASK

As a result of the colleague review and the pilot with students, the draft task will, no doubt, require some revision. This revision might be a major rewrite. More likely, it will be a minor revision in order to make the task clearer, less cumbersome, or differently slanted.

Once revised, the task is ready for the formal process of rubric design discussed in Chapter 6. However, teachers should be aware that the task may need further revision after the scoring rubric is written; that exercise frequently reveals inadequacies (usually minor) in the task itself.

SUMMARY

The process of task design has several steps, all of which should be completed. A performance task should not be used for actual assessment until it has been piloted with students. This suggests that at least a year will elapse between the decision to embark on a program of performance assessment and the implementation of such a system.

FIGURE 5.1 PERFORMANCE TASK DESIGN WORKSHEET

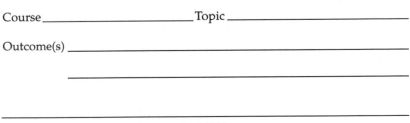

Course_____ Topic _____

Outcome(s) _____

_____

_____

Task Title

Brief description of the task (what students must do, and what product will result):

Directions to the students:

Criteria to be used to evaluate student responses:

FIGURE 5.2 PERFORMANCE TASK. AUTHENTIC SIMULATION

Outcome: _____

Topic: _____

You are (student or adult role or profession)

Who has been asked by (audience or superior)

To (accomplish a specific task)

Using (resources)

Under the constraints of (as found in such a situation)

Your work will be judged according to (criteria)

(Attach a rubric)

Based on Worksheets from the High Success Network and CLASS

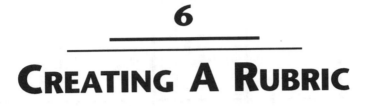

6

CREATING A RUBRIC

In order to use a performance task to evaluate student learning, a guide for evaluating student work, such as a rubric, is needed. The development of the task and the application of the rubric should be considered an iterative process (as each is developed and used, it suggests changes in the other) with the final combination of task and rubric evolving over time. This section includes guidance for the design of a rubric for a task.

DRAFTING A SCORING RUBRIC

Generally speaking, the criteria to be used in evaluating student work will have been identified in the course of developing a performance task. However, in order to convert these criteria into an actual scoring rubric, they must be elaborated and further defined. While holistic rubrics have their uses (e.g., in the summative evaluation of student work for awarding a diploma), this section will focus on the design of analytic rubrics. A general format for developing a rubric is provided in Figure 6.1.

GENERIC OR TASK-SPECIFIC?

The first question to be answered concerns the degree of task-specificity of the rubric. If, for example, the rubric is being developed for a group mathematics project, could the same rubric be used for other projects, or is its use confined to this particular one? Indeed, could the elements of the rubric,

FIGURE 6.1 PERFORMANCE RUBRIC

Criteria	(Activity)			
	1	2	3	4

concerned with making a group presentation, be used for other disciplines as well? Are there enough similarities between group presentations for mathematics, science, and social studies that the same evaluation guide could be used for all of them?

In general, of course, generic rubrics are more useful that task-specific ones. Creating rubrics is time-consuming and the more broadly they may be applied, the more useful and powerful they are. However, sometimes a common rubric will have to be adapted for use in other situations and in other disciplines; while many of the elements are the same, the ways in which they appear in student work are sufficiently different to warrant independent consideration.

TASK OR GENRE SPECIFIC, OR DEVELOPMENTAL

Another important question to be considered when creating a rubric is whether the rubric will be used on a single task (or a single type of task) or whether it will be used developmentally with students as they progress through many years of school. That is, will the rubric under development for a mathematics project, be applied for only this particular project which students do in the fourth grade, or could it be used also with students throughout the district, including those in the middle school as well as in high school?

If the rubric is to be used developmentally, it will probably have many more points on it, and the criteria may be written differently than if the rubric is to be used for a single task. A developmental rubric is useful for a school in which students have mathematics portfolios, and may be helpful in charting progress over time. However, a developmental rubric may not be as useful for any particular task as one created specifically for that task.

DETERMINING CRITERIA

Once the question of task-specificity or developmental rubric has been answered, the most important single step in creating a scoring rubric is to identify the criteria to be evaluated. The importance of attending carefully to this step cannot be overstated. It is in the determination of criteria that educators define important aspects of performance, and define, both for themselves and their students, what they mean by good quality. When defining criteria, several issues should be considered.

- *Type of criteria.* In mathematics, an essential criterion almost always concerns mathematical accuracy. Is the answer correct? Are computational errors major or minor? Are answers correctly labeled? Are all possible answers found?

  But in addition to computational accuracy, what else is important? What about conceptual understanding? Do students reveal, either through their approach to the problem or through the errors they make, that they have no understanding of the underlying concepts? Does the problem require a plan? If so, have students organized their information? Have they approached the problem in a systematic manner? Is the work presented neatly? Can a reader follow the student's line of reasoning?

In addition, a mathematics project might require that students collaborate together. How successfully do they do this? Do they establish a good division of labor, or do one or two students dominate the group? If the students make a presentation as part of the project, do they explain their thinking clearly? Are the other students interested in the presentation? Can they follow it? Is it engaging? It is important that the criteria identified for a task not consist only of those that are easiest to see, such as computational accuracy. The criteria should, taken together, define all the aspects of exemplary performance, even if some of them are somewhat challenging to specify and to evaluate.

One successful approach to the identification of criteria is to consider the task and to imagine an excellent student response to it. What would such a response include? The answer to that question can serve to identify important criteria. Alternatively, many teachers do the task themselves prior to assigning it to their students, creating, in effect, an exemplary response, and appreciating the issues inherent in the task for students.

- *Number and detail of criteria.* There is no single best answer to the question of "how many criteria?" Clearly, all important aspects of performance should be captured in the criteria. Moreover, those aspects of performance that are independent of one another should be designated as separate criteria.

It is possible to designate too many criteria, and for them to be too detailed. The resulting rubric is then cumbersome and time-consuming to use. On the other hand, a rubric that is too economical may not provide adequate information to students for them to improve performance. The number and level of detail of the rubric then, is partly a matter of how it is to be used and the age and skill level of the students. Rubrics used with special needs students, for example, are often made in great detail, so both teachers and students are aware of where improvement efforts should be focused.

- *Sub-criteria or elements.* Sometimes, several criteria are related to one another or one may be considered a sub-category of another. In that case, the criteria may contain within them sub-criteria or elements. For example, if students make a presentation as part of the mathematics project, the overall criterion might be "quality of presentation" with sub-criteria of "clarity," "originality and energy," and "involvement of all group members."

Occasionally, when educators think critically about the qualities they would look for in good student performance, they recognize that the task, as written, does not elicit those qualities; they then return to the task and alter the student directions. That is, students could do the task and not demonstrate the criteria that have been defined. In that case, the directions must be rewritten, or the task restructured, to elicit the desired performance.

NUMBER OF POINTS

The question of the number of points on a scoring scale is closely related, of course, to whether the rubric is task-specific or developmental. If developmental, it will almost certainly have more points than if it is task-specific, and the number of points should reflect the age range over which the rubric will be applied. For a skill, such as problem-solving or graphing, that develops from kindergarten through 12th grade, a scale with 10 points would be reasonable.

But even for task-specific rubrics, educators must decide on the number of points. As explained previously, an even number is preferable to an odd number, since it prevents the phenomenon known as "central tendency." But beyond that, there are several considerations to keep in mind.

- *Detail in distinctions.* With a larger number of points on a scale, fine distinctions are required when evaluating student work. While such detail can provide finely-tuned feedback to students, a rubric with many points is cumbersome and time-consuming to use. For practical purposes, a rubric with 4-6 points is recommended. The ones in this collection all contain four points.

- *Dividing line between acceptable and unacceptable performance.* It is helpful, at the outset, to determine the dividing line between acceptable and unacceptable performance. On a four-point scale, this line is either between the "1" and the "2" or between the "2" and the "3." That placement will be determined by where the greater detail is the more useful; that is, is it more useful to be able to specify degrees of inadequacy or degrees of adequacy?

- *General headings for different points.* The different points on the scale may be called simply by their numbers. On a four-point scale then, they would be 0, 1, 2, and 3 or 1, 2, 3, and 4. Or, they could be 10, 20, 30, and 40. Alternatively, the points can be given names such as "novice," "proficient," "exemplary," "great!" If this approach is taken, it is preferable to use positive, supportive words (such as "emerging") rather than negative ones (such as "inadequate").

DESCRIPTIONS OF LEVELS OF PERFORMANCE

Once the criteria and the number of scale points have been determined, it is time to actually write the descriptions of performance levels. Again, this step is critical and includes a number of factors.

- *The language used.* The words used to specify the qualities of different levels of performance should be descriptive, rather than comparative. For example, words such as "average" should be avoided. The descriptions of performance levels serve to further define the criteria, and are further defined themselves only when accompanied by actual samples of student work, called anchor papers.

- *All sub-criteria or elements defined.* If the criteria contain sub-criteria within them, each of these elements should be described in each of the performance descriptions. For example, if a criterion on presentation includes accuracy and originality, and involvement of all group members, then the descriptions for each of the levels should describe the group's presentation with respect to all those elements.

- *Distance between points.* To the extent possible, the distance between the points on a scale should be equal. That is, the distance between a "3" and a "4" should not be much greater than that between a "2" and a "3."

- *The line between acceptable and unacceptable performance.* Placement of the line between acceptable and unacceptable performance should receive particular scrutiny. While the highest and lowest levels of performance are the easiest to describe, those in the middle, that define acceptable and unacceptable performance, are the most important. It is here, after all, that educators define their standards and specify the quality of work on which they insist and expect mastery. It is recommended that this level be described with particular care.

SUMMARY

The most critical step in the development of a scoring rubric for evaluating student performance is its initial design. For this process, a number of factors — such as whether it is generic or specific, the actual criteria, the number of points on the scale, and the language used to define the points — must be taken into account.

PILOTING THE RUBRIC WITH STUDENT WORK

The proof of a rubric is in its use with student work, and not until a rubric is used to evaluate actual student work will its authors know whether it is viable. Several steps are recommended.

EVALUATING A SAMPLE OF STUDENT WORK

A good place to begin is to collect a small number of samples (about 8) of students' work, representing the full range of probable responses in the class. The sample should include those students from whom the best work would be expected, as well as those whose work might not be adequate. If possible, the pieces of work should be anonymous; they could be numbered and referred to by their numbers.

Then, with the rubric in hand, evaluate the student work using the draft rubric. The form shown in Fig. 6.2 may be used, with the criteria listed (or numbered) down the side, and the levels of performance for different students specified in the column corresponding to each one. Surveying the entire page then, provides a summary of the levels of performance represented by the class as a whole, and can offer guidance as to the next instructional steps that may be needed.

FIGURE 6.2 PERFORMANCE ASSESSMENT EVALUATION RESULTS

Evaluator _____ Date _____

Task _____ Grade Level _____

Student Criteria	Student 1	Student 2	Student 3	Student 4	Student 5	Student 6	Student 7	Student 8

INTER-RATER AGREEMENT

Even with careful design, it is possible that the rubric or the use of the rubric, is not yet reliable. The only way to check this is to request assistance from a colleague. It is recommended that another educator be introduced to the task and the rubric, and be provided with the same sample of student work initially used. This person should then evaluate the same students, and assign scores on each criterion based on the draft rubric.

Scores for each student on each criterion should then be compared. Clearly, the goal is for all scores to be the same, although this is unlikely to occur. Any discrepancies should then be discussed until the cause of the discrepancy is understood; most frequently, discrepancies are caused by a lack of clarity in the words used in the performance levels.

REVISING THE RUBRIC (AND POSSIBLY ALSO THE TASK)

As a result of evaluating student work and of comparing scores assigned with those of another educator, it is likely that the rubric (and possibly also the task) will require some revision. With luck, these revisions will not be extensive and will serve to clarify points of ambiguity.

LOCATING ANCHOR PAPERS

As a final step in rubric design, samples of student work that represent different points on the scale on each of the different criteria should be identified. By keeping these from year to year, it is possible to chart the course of general improvement of student work over time. In addition, only through the use of anchor papers can educators be sure that their standards are remaining the same, and are not subject to a gradual drift.

SUMMARY

Not until a scoring rubric has been piloted with actual student papers will its designers know whether it will prove to be effective.

INVOLVING STUDENTS IN RUBRIC DESIGN AND USE

Many educators find that one of the most powerful uses of performance tasks and rubrics is to engage students actively in their design and use. That aspect of work with rubrics is described in this section, which may be used productively even with elementary students.

ADVANTAGES

Many advantages are cited for engaging students in the design of scoring rubrics. First and most important, by participating in the design of a scoring rubric, students are absolutely clear on the criteria by which their work will be evaluated. Furthermore, many teachers discover that students have good ideas to contribute to a rubric; they know, for example, the characteristics of an exemplary mathematics project.

But more importantly, when students know at the outset the criteria by which their work will be evaluated, and when they know the description of exemplary performance, they are better able (and more motivated) to produce high-quality work. The rubric provides guidance as to quality; students know exactly what they must do.

Consequently, many teachers find that when they involve students in the use of scoring rubrics, the quality of student work improves dramatically. So, when teachers have anchors (e.g., exemplary projects from a previous year) to illustrate good quality work to students, the general standard of work produced improves from year to year.

A PLAN FOR ACTION

It is not obvious just how to engage students in designing and using scoring rubrics for evaluating student work. Some suggestions are offered here.

- *Starting with a draft.* A discussion with students about scoring rubrics should begin with a draft rubric already prepared by the teacher. The teacher should have some ideas, at least in general terms, of the criteria that should emerge from the discussion. Then, while students may suggest original ideas, the teacher can be sure that the final product includes all important aspects of performance.

Students may be asked to contribute both to the generation of criteria and to the writing of performance descriptions. Many teachers are pleasantly surprised with the level of sophistication demonstrated by their students in this endeavor.

The teacher should maintain control of the process of rubric design. While students will have excellent ideas, which should be accommodated to the maximum extent possible, the teacher should never relinquish control of the project to students.

- *Student self-assessment.* The first type of student use of a scoring rubric should be for students to evaluate their own work. Most teachers find that their students are, generally speaking, quite hard on themselves, in some cases more so than their teachers would be. Of course, clear performance descriptions will help in keeping evaluations consistent, but students frequently reveal a genuine concern for maintaining high standards, even when evaluating their own work.

- *Peer assessment.* When the climate in a class is sufficiently supportive, students may be able to engage in peer assessment. Such an activity requires a high level of trust among students. However, if students have participated in the design of a scoring rubric, and have used it to evaluate their own work, they will generally be able to provide feedback to their peers in the same spirit of caring and support. When that occurs, the classroom becomes transformed into a true community of learners.

SUMMARY

The most powerful use of scoring rubrics derives from engaging students in their design and use. However, such participation by students is likely to evolve over time.

7

ADAPTING EXISTING PERFORMANCE TASKS AND RUBRICS

Frequently, much time and effort may be saved by adapting an existing task, with its scoring rubric, to one's own use. Through this approach, educators can benefit from the work of others, and still have a task that reflects their own unique needs.

There are many sources of existing performance tasks that may be adapted, in addition to those in this book. Many textbook publishers now offer some performance tasks and rubrics as part of their package. Some state departments of education have also created prototype tasks. And the National Council of Teachers of Mathematics (NCTM) has published some examples. The techniques for adapting existing tasks are described in this section.

MATCHING OUTCOMES, TOPICS, AND STUDENTS

The first step in identifying tasks suitable for adaptation is to match the outcomes and topics assessed by the task with those in one's own curriculum. The performance tasks in this book have been aligned with the strands developed by the New Standards Project, and with different topics found in most mathematics curricula. By examining those alignments, educators can determine whether a given task would be of value to them in assessing student mastery of their own curriculum.

It is unlikely that such a match will be perfect. Frequently, a performance task will ask students to perform an operation or complete an activity that students in a given class have not yet learned. Alternatively, a scoring rubric will include criteria that do not reflect a district's curriculum. In those cases, either the task or the rubric will have to be adjusted.

Also, a particular task might have been developed with students in mind who are very different from one's own class. In order for a task to be effective, it must be one that students can relate to.

SUMMARY

In order to determine whether a performance task can be used as written, educators must match the task's outcomes and topics with those in their curriculum, and consider their own students.

ADJUSTING THE TASK

The actual task may need adaptation, either to reflect a school's curriculum, to make it more meaningful and relevant to the students concerned, or to adjust the situation to local conditions. Each of these situations will be considered separately in this section.

TO REFLECT A SCHOOL'S CURRICULUM

If there is poor alignment between a performance task and a school's curriculum, the task must be adjusted to correct the mismatch. Such an adjustment will take the form of adding to or subtracting from, or simply changing, the requirements for the students. For example, a particular task might require students to find an average of a group of numbers as one step in solving a problem. If students in a particular class have not yet learned how to do that, the task should be adjusted so that such a step is not needed.

Alternatively, one school's curriculum might teach estimation in the course of work in measurement, while a performance task involving measurement does not, as written, ask the students to estimate their answer before measuring and calculating. In that case, adapting the task might involve adding a step which requires the students to estimate.

TO REFLECT A GROUP OF STUDENTS

Sometimes a task is designed with the characteristics of a group of students in mind, and it is not ideally suited to others. Different classes of students are not identical in the sophistication of their thinking, and in the knowledge and skills they bring to a class. Therefore, a performance task that is to be used with any group of students must be considered with the characteristics of that class in mind.

This factor will often be reflected in the amount of scaffolding provided to students as they solve problems. For lower-functioning students, a task might have to be written with more "tips" for solution than would be needed for more advanced students. Alternatively, a single task might be broken into several sub-tasks that students work on separately.

On the other hand, a task can be made more difficult and cognitively complex. A task that asks students simply to find an answer can be adjusted to require, in addition, an explanation of why a certain approach was employed. Or, a task that includes many suggestions for students as to how to proceed could be rewritten with just the question, with few or no "tips" to the student. Each of these efforts will make the task more challenging, and may make it suitable for an advanced group of students.

If a performance task is adjusted to reflect a group of students, particularly if it is deliberately made more or less challenging, it should be adapted purposefully and the changes noted when student progress is monitored. If, for example, a task is deliberately simplified for a group of students, it should be clear to any reader of those students' records that the curriculum outcomes on which they were evaluated were somewhat different from those of another group of students.

TO ENHANCE ITS RELEVANCE

Another type of adaptation that might be warranted is that which makes a performance task more suitable to a local situation, and therefore more relevant and meaningful to a group of students. For example, a task might ask students to calculate the amount of money they could earn by recycling their household cans, bottles, and plastic containers. If, however, steel cans and plastic cannot be recycled in a particular area, it might be a good idea to revise the task so it concerns only aluminum cans and glass bottles.

Alternatively, an entire situation might be changed to reflect local conditions. For instance, a performance task might concern calculating the floor area of a school's classrooms for the purpose of recommending the purchase of carpeting. If, however, the school is about to have all its walls painted, the students could make those calculations instead, and actually make a presentation of their findings to the maintenance department of the school district. Such efforts to enhance relevance and authenticity pay big dividends in enhancing student engagement in the task.

SUMMARY

A performance task may be adjusted to make it more reflective of the school's curriculum, or more suitable to a group of students, or to reflect conditions in a particular setting.

ADJUSTING THE RUBRIC

If a task is adjusted to reflect a district's curriculum, to be more suitable to a group of students, or to be made more relevant, the rubric will probably also require adaptation. The extent to which such adaptation is needed will depend, of course, on the amount of adjustment to the task itself.

ADAPTING THE CRITERIA

If the task is changed, the criteria may no longer apply. The task may now encourage students to exhibit knowledge, skill, or understanding that were not part of the original task. If so, criteria related to these features should be added. Alternatively, elements of the original task may have been dropped; if so, the criteria corresponding to those elements should be eliminated.

ADJUSTING THE PERFORMANCE DESCRIPTIONS

When a task is changed, particularly if the evaluation criteria are also changed, the performance descriptions may require adjustment. Occasionally, the performance descriptions need adjustment even with no change in the task itself.

- If the level of difficulty of a task has been changed, either by altering the cognitive demands of the directions or by splitting it into several discrete tasks, the performance descriptions for even the same criteria may no longer be suitable. The descriptions may require revision to reflect the changed demands of the revised task.

- Even if the task has not been changed, but is being used with students who are more or less advanced than those for whom it was designed, the performance descriptions may need revision. Sometimes this can be accomplished by simply shifting the descriptions one place to the right, or the left; that is, the description that was a "3" is now a "2," that which was a "4" is now the "3," and a new description is written for the "4."

- If the task has been revised to reflect a particular situation (for example, calculating floor area for carpeting instead of wall area for paint), the performance descriptions may need revising to reflect the changes. On the other hand, they may not need revision, depending on how they were written in the first place. Clearly, the more generic they are, the less revision will be needed. But if the rubric has been written to be highly task-specific, substantial changes will be needed to reflect a different context.

SUMMARY

If a performance task is adjusted to make it more suitable for a group of students, its scoring rubric will almost certainly require a parallel change. Even if the task is not changed, educators may find that they want to adjust the rubric to better match the skills of their students, or the criteria important to them.

PILOTING WITH STUDENTS

No adaptation of a performance task and its rubric is complete without trying it with students. Generally, all performance tasks (even those that are not adaptations of existing tasks) are revised somewhat after this pilot; certainly the scoring rubrics are revised in light of actual student work. The questions to be answered as a result of this pilot are summarized below.

ENGAGEMENT AND AUTHENTICITY

Are students engaged in the task? In the course of revision, did the task become irrelevant and boring to students? If possible, does the task reflect authentic applications of knowledge and skill?

ELICITING DESIRED KNOWLEDGE AND SKILL

Does the task, as revised, elicit the desired knowledge and skill from students? Occasionally, when tasks are revised, they lose their essential nature, so students complete the task without demonstrating the critical knowledge and skill about which their teachers are interested. This is most likely to happen if the student directions have been substantially revised.

CLARITY OF STUDENT DIRECTIONS

Are the directions to the students clear? In particular, if student's work will be evaluated according to specific criteria, have students been informed, in some manner, of those criteria in the directions themselves?

INDIVIDUAL ASSESSMENT

Does the task still permit the assessment of individual students? Or have the teachers, in the interests of making the task more relevant to a particular group of students or a unique situation, also introduced group work that obscures the contribution of individuals?

TECHNICAL FEATURES OF THE RUBRIC

Does the scoring rubric, as revised, still meet all the technical requirements described in Chapter 6? Do the descriptions of levels of performance use vivid words, and avoid comparative language? Are the distances between points on the scale approximately equal? Do the criteria reflect the most important aspects of performance?

Only an actual pilot of the revised task will elicit unambiguous answers to these questions. As educators and their students become more experienced in the use of performance tasks, however, this step may be combined with the first actual use of the task to evaluate student learning. That is, the task may be adapted as needed and used with students. Then, if it becomes apparent that the adaptation did not avoid all the pitfalls described above, the actual scores awarded to students can be adjusted accordingly. For example, if student performance is poor, but it becomes clear that the principal reason for the poor performance relates to lack of clarity in the directions, then the teacher's evaluation of student mastery must reflect that difficulty.

SUMMARY

The final step in adapting an existing performance task and rubric is its actual pilot with students. Only then can educators be sure that it accomplishes their desired purposes.

8

Upper Elementary School Mathematics Performance Tasks

In this section of the book you will find a collection of performance tasks and rubrics aligned to the mathematics standards, and addressing all the important topics in elementary school mathematics. They are arranged in alphabetical order (by title), with a table at the beginning of the chapter to assist you in locating tasks you may want to assess specific skills and concepts. Some of the tasks include student work, which serves both to illustrate the manner in which students interpret the directions given to them and to anchor the different points in the scoring rubrics.

You may find that the tasks are useful to you as presented. Alternatively, you may find that they can serve your purposes better if you adapt them somewhat. One way of adapting tasks is to incorporate names of people and places familiar to students in your class. This practice is frequently amusing to students, and therefore engaging.

In addition, tasks may be simplified or made more difficult by increasing or decreasing the amount of structure (or scaffolding) you provide to students. When you, the teacher, give guidance to students by outlining the steps needed in a solution, the resulting task is significantly easier (and less authentic.) Similarly, for those tasks that are provided with considerable scaffolding, you can make them more complex by removing it.

Standard / Task	Number Operations Computation	Geometry Measurement
Dice Toss		
Dog Food	X	
Fencing		X
Flowers	X	X
Fraction Facts	X	
Garden Fence	X	X
Make a Number	X	
Making Change	X	
Outfits	X	X
Packing Tape	X	X
Party Planning	X	
Party Prizes	X	
Peanuts	X	
Pet Survey		
Pieces of Pizza	X	X
Pizza Choices	X	
Sale Price	X	
School Play	X	
School Supplies	X	
Science Fair	X	X
Spinning Advantage	X	X
Vending Value	X	
Wheels	X	
Write a Story	X	

Statistics Probability	Reasoning, Problem Solving	Mathematical Skills and Tools	Mathematics Communication
X	X	X	X
	X	X	X
	X	X	X
	X	X	X
	X	X	X
	X	X	X
	X	X	
X	X	X	X
X	X	X	X
	X	X	X
	X	X	X
	X	X	X
	X	X	X
X	X	X	X
	X	X	X
X	X	X	X
X	X	X	X
	X	X	X
	X	X	X
	X	X	X
X	X	X	X
X	X	X	X
X	X	X	X
	X	X	X

DICE TOSS

MATHEMATICS STANDARDS ASSESSED

- Problem solving and mathematical reasoning
- Statistics and probability
- Mathematical skills and tools, and
- Mathematical communication.

DIRECTIONS TO THE STUDENT

William is tossing two number cubes, each with the numbers 1 through 6. He has bet his friend Tony that if they each toss the cubes the same number of times he can toss a "7" more times than Tony can toss a "5." Tony has asked for your advice as to whether he should accept the bet. What do you think? Write him a short letter explaining why he should or should not accept William's bet, and why.

MATHEMATICAL CONCEPT

In this task students must determine the different combinations for a "5" and a "7," and recognize that since there are more ways to toss a "7" than a "5" the chances are greater for a "7."

SOLUTION

With two number cubes, each numbered 1 through 6, there are 36 possible combinations. Of those 36 combinations, there are four ways to make a "5": 1,4; 4,1; 2,3; and 3,2. On the other hand, there are six ways to make a "7": 1,6; 6,1; 2,5; 5,2; 3,4; 4,3. William can expect to toss a "7" once out of every 6 times he tosses the cubes (6 out of 36) whereas Tony could expect to toss a "5" only once out of each nine tosses (4 out of 36). Tony would be ill advised, therefore, to accept William's bet.

SCORING GUIDE

	Level One	Level Two	Level Three	Level Four
Mathematical Accuracy	Cannot identify all the ways to toss the dice or to make a "7" or a "5."	Identifies most of the ways to toss the dice and to make a "5" and a "7." No calculation of the odds of tossing a "5" or a "7."	Identifies virtually all the ways to toss the dice and to make a "5" and a "7." Attempt at calculation of the odds for a "5" and a "7."	Identifies all the ways to toss the dice and to make a "5" and a "7;" correctly calculates the odds of tossing a "5" and a "7."
Approach	Random and disorganized; no systematic approach.	Some system apparent in the approach; however, it is difficult to follow.	Systematic and organized approach, but not well presented.	Highly systematic and organized approach; neatly and clearly presented.
Explanation	Little or no explanation, or impossible to follow.	Explanation attempted, but difficult to understand.	Explanation fairly clear, but thinking process not always easy to follow..	Explanation very clear, and thinking process easy to follow.

DOG FOOD

MATHEMATICS STANDARDS ASSESSED

- Number operations and concepts
- Problem solving and mathematical reasoning
- Mathematical skills and tools, and
- Mathematical communication

DIRECTIONS TO THE STUDENT

Kathy's family has two dogs, Charlie and Spot. Charlie is a big dog and eats a whole can of dog food each day. Spot is smaller and eats only 2/3 of a can each day. If dog food costs $2.00 for three cans, how much will it cost Kathy's family to feed the dogs each month (30 days)? You may draw pictures to assist you.

Show your work clearly, so another person could tell how you arrived at your answer.

MATHEMATICAL CONCEPT

This task requires students to multiply simple fractions and to calculate a total. But since the task involves numbers of cans of dog food as well as money, it requires several steps. The task may be made somewhat simpler by saying that Spot eats 1/2 can of dog food each day.

SOLUTION

Charlie will eat 30 cans of dog food in the month, whereas Spot will eat 20 cans (2/3 x 30). Therefore, Kathy's family will need to buy 50 cans of dog food. Since 3 cans of food costs $2.00, 51 cans would cost $34 (17 x $2.00). But since they need only 50 cans, the total cost is $33.34 ($34.00 - $0.66 –- the cost of a single can of food.)

Alternatively, one could argue that since Charlie will eat 30 cans of dog food in the month, his food will cost $20.00. Since Spot will eat 20 cans, that will cost $12.00 (6 x 3 = 18 cans; and

3 cans costs $2.00) + $.1.34 (the cost of two cans of dog food at 3 cans for $2.00) or $13.34. The total for the two dogs, then is $20.00 + $13.34 or $33.34.

SCORING GUIDE

	Level One	Level Two	Level Three	Level Four
Mathematical Accuracy	Major computational errors reflecting inability to perform necessary operations.	Some calculations performed correctly, but others not accurate, leading to error.	Appropriate operation(s) selected; few mathematical errors, leading to mostly accurate conclusions.	Correct operations chosen, with no computational errors in either multiplication of fractions or addition.
Approach	Random and disorganized; no systematic approach.	Some system apparent in the approach; however, it is difficult to follow.	Systematic and organized approach, but not well presented.	Highly systematic and organized approach; neatly and clearly presented.

LEVEL ONE

$$\begin{array}{r} 10 \\ + 10 \\ \hline 70 \end{array}$$

$20.00
because $10.00
dollars for the
Big dog and
the little dog
was 10 so it
is $70.00.

This response indicates poor understanding of the problem and provides little sense that the student has a method for solving it. The student has, apparently, grouped the cans of dog food into clusters of three, but does not go further. The answer provided is very far from correct, and there is no indication of how it was calculated.

LEVEL ONE

I can a day

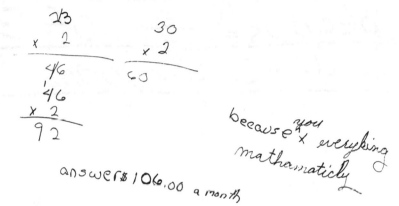

$$
\begin{array}{r}
23 \\
\times \ 2 \\
\hline
46
\end{array}
$$

$$
\begin{array}{r}
30 \\
\times \ 2 \\
\hline
60
\end{array}
$$

$$
\begin{array}{r}
46 \\
\times \ 2 \\
\hline
92
\end{array}
$$

answer $106.00 a month

because you x everyking mathamaticly

This response provides no indication of how the answer was
arrived at, and offers as an explanation only that "you multiply
everything mathematically." This student has probably not
fully understood the question.

LEVEL TWO

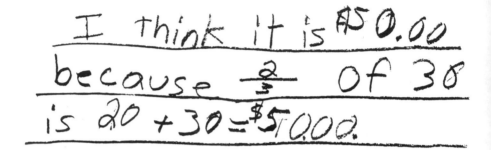

I think it is $50.00
because $\frac{2}{3}$ of 30
is 20 + 30 = $50.00

This student correctly determines that the two dogs together
will consume 50 cans of food in the month. However, the cost
of the dog food is not included in the solution.

LEVEL TWO

Kathy's family has two dogs, Charlie and Spot. Charlie is a big dog and eats a whole can of dog food each day. Spot is smaller and eats only 2/3 of a can each day. If dog food costs $2.00 for three cans, how much will it cost Kathy's family to feed the dogs each month (30 days)? You may draw pictures to assist you.

$$\begin{array}{r} \text{×} \\ \$1.50 \\ \times\ 30 \\ \hline 145.00 \end{array}$$

Show your work clearly, so another person could tell how you arrived at your answer.

$$\begin{array}{r} 2.00 \\ \times\ 30 \\ \hline \$60.00 \end{array}$$

I figured out that it would be $15.00 because if Charlie can eat one whole can and spot eats one can so you have to figure out how much two cans are and multiply it by thirty.

This response indicates a sense of the complexity of the situation, and makes an attempt to accommodate it. However, the answer is incorrect, and does not seem to include both the number of cans of dog food needed and their cost.

LEVEL THREE

This response represents a low "3." The student shows an understanding of the problem, and the answer is close to being correct. The drawings indicate that the student has accommodated both the amount of food eaten and the cost of the food. However, the explanation is not very clear.

LEVEL THREE

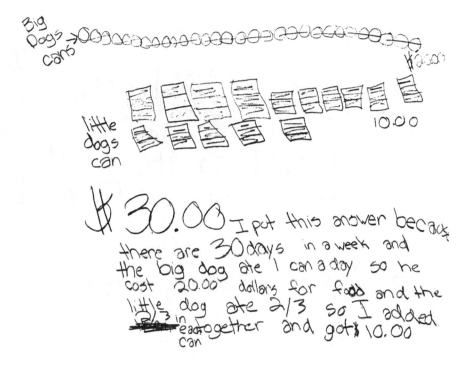

Big
Dogs
cans →

little
dogs
can

10.00

$ 30.00 I put this answer because
there are 30 days in a week and
the big dog ate 1 can a day so he
cost 20.00 dollars for food and the
little dog ate 2/3 so I added
~~2/3 in~~ each together and got $ 10.00
can

This response is close to the correct answer, and demonstrates
clear understanding of the situation. However, the actual solution is not quite successful since the student loses sight of the
different factors.

LEVEL FOUR

Spot eats 2 cans every 3 day,
and Charlie 3. Charlie
costs $2.00 for 3 days and
Spot is 1.32 so it's 3.32 per
3 days or 33.20 for a month.

This response approaches the problem in an interesting way, by calculating the amount per day to feed both dogs. The approach is a successful one, and yields the correct answer.

LEVEL FOUR

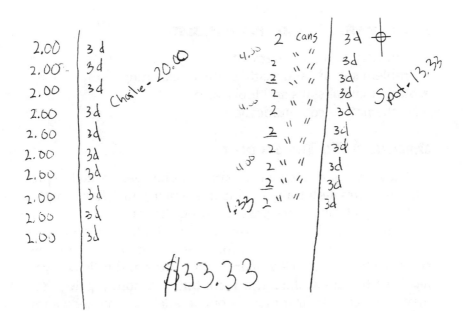

This approach calculates the cost of food for the two dogs separately, and then combines them together. The solution is a little difficult to follow, but it is accurate.

FENCING

MATHEMATICS STANDARDS ASSESSED

- Geometry and measurement
- Problem solving and mathematical reasoning
- Mathematical skills and tools, and
- Mathematical communication

DIRECTIONS TO THE STUDENT

You work for a fencing company that has been asked to prepare an estimate for a job. You use fencing in 4 foot lengths, with two rails and fence posts holding the rails (see the drawing below.) You have been asked to build a fence for a farmer to enclose a rectangular field for cows. The field has dimensions of 600' x 300'. How many fence posts and rails will you need for the job, if the fence were built without a gate? You may use a calculator if there is one available. Prepare a summary of the requirements for fencing material, to present to the president of the company.

As an extension, can you write a rule for determining, for any length of fence, how many rails and posts you would need?

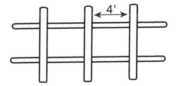

MATHEMATICAL CONCEPT

In this task, students must recognize that the number of rails needed for a length of fencing is twice the number of fence posts. In addition, students must determine the perimeter of the field and perform the appropriate mathematical calculations. The extension question asks students to discern the pattern for solving all such problems.

This task is adapted from one presented in *Measuring Up: Prototypes for Mathematics Assessment.*

SOLUTION

The total perimeter of the field is 2 x 600 + 2 x 300 or 1800 feet. The number of sections needed is 1800 (4 = 450). The number of rails needed is 450 x 2 = 900. The number of posts needed is 450.

SCORING GUIDE

	Level One	Level Two	Level Three	Level Four
Mathematical Accuracy and Use of Calculator	Inappropriate operation(s) selected, and/or many errors, leading to wildly erroneous conclusions.	Mixture of appropriate and inappropriate operation(s); some errors, but allowing largely for accurate conclusions.	Appropriate operation(s) selected; virtually no mathematical errors; with accurate conclusions.	In addition, the work shows evidence of advanced planning.
Approach	Random and disorganized; no systematic approach.	Some system apparent in the approach; however, it is difficult to follow.	Systematic and organized approach, but not well presented.	Highly systematic and organized approach; neatly and clearly presented.
Summary	Summary not presented of impossible to follow.	Explanation attempted, but difficult to understand.	Explanation fairly clear, but thinking process not always easy to follow.	Explanation very clear, and thinking process easy to follow.

FLOWER PLANTING

MATHEMATICS STANDARDS ASSESSED

- Number operations and concepts
- Geometry and measurement
- Problem solving and mathematical reasoning
- Mathematical skills and tools, and
- Mathematical communication

DIRECTIONS TO THE STUDENT

In your town, a group of citizens has decided to make a huge circular flower bed in the center of town, and they have been planting bulbs in the bed. The drawing below shows where the bulbs have already been planted, and they need your help in determining how many more bulbs to buy. They have already planted 4000 bulbs.

Determine how many more bulbs they will need to complete the flower bed, and write a brief description of how you found your answer.

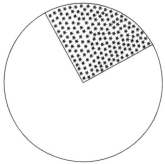

MATHEMATICAL CONCEPT

In this task, students must determine what proportion of the whole has been planted, and therefore how many more bulbs will be needed. They must also apply an intuitive knowledge of ratios and geometry.

This task is adapted from one developed by the Kentucky Department of Education.

SOLUTION

The portion of the flower bed that has been planted is approximately one-fourth. Therefore, since 4000 bulbs were needed for one-fourth of the bed, about 16,000 bulbs would be required for the entire bed, or 12,000 more bulbs.

SCORING GUIDE

	Level One	Level Two	Level Three	Level Four
Conceptual Understanding	The solution exhibits little or no understanding of the situation.	The solution exhibits limited understanding of the situation.	The solution exhibits good understanding of the situation.	The solution exhibits thorough understanding of the situation.
Mathematical Accuracy	Serious computational errors, leading to erroneous conclusions.	Minor computational errors, but allowing largely for accurate conclusions.	Computations performed accurately, by series of additions.	Computations performed accurately, using multiplication.
Explanation	Little or no explanation, or impossible to follow.	Explanation attempted, but difficult to understand.	Explanation fairly clear, but thinking process not always easy to follow.	Explanation very clear, and thinking process easy to follow.

FRACTION FACTS

MATHEMATICS STANDARDS ASSESSED

- Number operations and concepts
- Problem solving and mathematical reasoning
- Mathematical skills and tools, and
- Mathematical communication

DIRECTIONS TO THE STUDENT

Below are five fractions:

$$\frac{1}{4} \qquad \frac{1}{3} \qquad \frac{1}{9} \qquad \frac{1}{2} \qquad \frac{1}{12}$$

1. Write the fractions in order from smallest to largest.

2. Jose told Chris that for fractions with a "1" in the numerator - the top, the larger the number in the denominator - the bottom - the smaller the fraction. Is Jose correct about this? How do you know?

MATHEMATICAL CONCEPT

This task requires students to understand the inverse relationship between the size of numbers in the denominator of a unit fraction and the value of that fraction.

SOLUTION

The correct sequence for the fractions is as follows:

$$\frac{1}{12} \qquad \frac{1}{9} \qquad \frac{1}{4} \qquad \frac{1}{3} \qquad \frac{1}{2}$$

It can be seen that as the numbers in the denominator become smaller, the fraction itself becomes larger. The student's explanation should include explicit recognition of this inverse relationship, and that as the number of pieces something is divided into increases, the size of each piece decreases.

SCORING GUIDE

	Level One	Level Two	Level Three	Level Four
Ordering of Fractions	Fractions ordered inaccurately.	A few of the fractions are placed in the correct sequence.	Most of the fractions are placed in the correct sequence.	All of the fractions are placed in the correct sequence.
Explanation	No explanation given, or impossible to follow.	Explanation includes no explicit recognition of the relationship between the size of the number in the denominator and the size of the fraction.	Explanation includes only partial explicit recognition of the relationship between the size of the number in the denominator and the size of the fraction.	Explanation includes explicit recognition of the relationship between the size of the number in the denominator and the size of the fraction.

GARDEN FENCE

MATHEMATICS STANDARDS ASSESSED

- Number operations and concepts
- Geometry and measurement
- Problem solving and mathematical reasoning
- Mathematical skills and tools, and
- Mathematical communication

DIRECTIONS TO THE STUDENT

Elizabeth has decided to plant a rectangular flower garden with 24 plants. The plants need to be 1 foot apart. She also knows that the rabbits like to eat young plants, so she has decided to put up a fence around her garden.

Elizabeth does not want to buy more fencing than she has to, and she thinks it might matter how she plants the garden. What do you think? How should Elizabeth plant her garden so she needs the least amount of fencing? Show your answer in pictures and in words.

MATHEMATICAL CONCEPT

This task concerns the relationship of area and perimeter and requires that students determine the different ways 24 plants can be arranged, and the perimeter of each arrangement. Some students may not initially recognize that the fencing requirements for the different configurations are different.

SOLUTION

There are four possible ways to arrange 24 plants in a rectangle. These arrangements, and their perimeters are:

Configuration	Perimeter
1 x 24	50 feet
2 x 12	28 feet
3 x 8	22 feet
4 x 6	20 feet

From this table, it is apparent that the most "efficient" arrangement, the one that uses the least amount of fencing, is to place the plants in four rows of six plants each or six rows of four plants each.

SCORING GUIDE

	Level One	Level Two	Level Three	Level Four
Mathematical Accuracy	Does not identify all the possible configurations for the plants, nor the correct perimeter of each one.	Identifies most of the possible configurations for the plants, correctly calculates the perimeter of some of them.	Identifies all of the possible configurations for the plants, correctly calculates the perimeter of all of them.	In addition, correctly concludes that the 4 x 6 configuration uses the least amount of fencing.
Approach	Random and disorganized; no systematic approach.	Some system apparent in the approach; however, it is difficult to follow.	Systematic and organized approach, but not well presented.	Highly systematic and organized approach, neatly and clearly presented.
Drawing	Very disorganized and messy; impossible to identify the different configurations.	Different configurations attempted, but difficult to follow.	All the configurations included in the drawing, but not neatly presented.	All the configurations included in the drawing, but not neatly presented.
Explanation	Little or no explanation, or impossible to follow.	Explanation attempted, but difficult to understand.	Explanation fairly clear, but thinking process not always easy to follow.	Explanation very clear, and thinking process easy to follow.

MAKE A NUMBER

MATHEMATICS STANDARDS ASSESSED

- Number operations and concepts
- Problem solving and mathematical reasoning
- Mathematical skills and tools, and

DIRECTIONS TO THE STUDENT

How many ways can you make 25? Use all the operations you have learned.

Note: these directions may be varied to ask students to make different numbers, or to use particular operations. A certain number of answers may also be specified.

MATHEMATICAL CONCEPT

This task invites students to use what they have learned about the different operations, order of operations, and the use of parentheses to "make" a given number. They can also recognize patterns in the addition and subtraction facts to come up with a large number of different ways to make a single number.

Note: some teachers use this as an instructional activity every day, in which students make the date in as many ways as possible.

SOLUTION

There are an infinite number of possible answers to the question. For example, using only addition, students could offer $1 + 24, 2 + 23, 3 + 22$, etc. Using only subtraction, there are even more possibilities: $26 - 1$; $27 - 2$; $28 - 3$; $29 - 4$, etc. Using some multiplication, one could propose $(3 \times 4) + 13$, or $2(3 \times 4) + 1$. Division could be used, as in $100 \div 4$, or $(80 \div 4) + 5$. Even more exotic answers could use square roots, if these have been learned.

SCORING GUIDE

	Level One	Level Two	Level Three	Level Four
Mathematical Accuracy	Many computational error.	Only a few computational errors, but a narrow range of operations used and only a few answers given.	No computational errors; a moderate number of solutions provided using most operations known.	No computational errors; a large number of solutions provided using all known operations.
Approach	Random and disorganized; no systematic approach to finding many solutions.	Some patterns attempted in the approach; however, it is difficult to follow.	Clear use of patterns in the finding of answers, but not clearly presented.	Highly systematic and organized approach; neatly and clearly presented.

MAKING CHANGE

MATHEMATICS STANDARDS ASSESSED

- Number operations and concepts
- Problem solving and mathematical reasoning
- Statistics and probability
- Mathematical skills and tools, and
- Mathematical communication

DIRECTIONS TO THE STUDENT

Lynn had only quarters, dimes and nickels to buy her lunch. She spent all her money and received no change. Could she have spent $1.98? Explain how you know.

MATHEMATICAL CONCEPT

In this task students must demonstrate understanding of how sums are made with US coins, in particular that with no pennies, all sums spent must be multiples of 5. Only with pennies is it possible to make $1.98.

This task is adapted from one developed for the National Assessment of Educational Progress (NAEP).

SOLUTION

Unlike many performance tasks, this one has a single correct answer. The answer to the question is "no," that Lynn could not have spent $1.98 with only quarters, dimes and nickels. The reason given must include explicit recognition that in order to make $1.98 Lynn would have needed three pennies, which she does not have.

SCORING GUIDE

	Level One	Level Two	Level Three	Level Four
Mathematical Accuracy	States that Lynn could have spent $1.98.	Response states that Lynn might have been able to spend $1.98.	States that Lynn could not have spent $1.98.	Emphatically states that Lynn could have spent $1.98.
Explanation	Explanation muddled; no mention of needing three pennies.	Explanation suggests the need for pennies, but unclear.	Explanation states that pennies are needed, but with no reason given.	Explanation states that pennies are needed, with the correct reason given.

LEVEL ONE

Yes, because there some
quarters ands some dimes
and some nickel might
equal up to $1.98.

This response indicates poor understanding of the value of US coins, and, furthermore, offers a somewhat confused explanation.

LEVEL TWO

no, she could of, but she could have had the right amount and didn't no it.

4 quarters
9 dimes
1 nickels
and maybe
3 pennies

This response is difficult to interpret without additional conversation with the student. As written, it provides little conclusive evidence that the student completely understands that Lynn needs 3 pennies to make $1.98. However, it is ambiguous, and the student's understanding may be greater than indicated.

LEVEL THREE

She couldn't have the nickels isn't so

4 quatters = 1.00

9 pime = $1.90

now the nickles goes 5 10 15 already
past the 8¢.

This response indicates understanding of the principle that
pennies are needed to make $1.98. However, the explanation is
a little unclear, relying on the skip counting by fives to make
the argument.

LEVEL THREE

No she couldn't because she
she didn't have 4 quarters, 9 dimes, 8 pennies

This response indicates understanding of the need for pennies to make $1.98. However, it demonstrates a lack of flexibility in how to combine coins, suggesting that the only way to make $1.98 is with 4 quarters, 9 dimes, and 8 pennies.

LEVEL FOUR

No, because if you use dimes, nickles, and quarters you would have to get a answer with a 5 on the end of it or a zero on the end of it if you wanted to get that number you would pennies.

This response draws on knowledge of number theory to answer the question correctly. Since $1.98 does not end in a "5" or a "0" pennies must be needed.

LEVEL FOUR

No. She would need pennies
to spend $1.98

This response, while not elegantly stated, indicates clear understanding of the need for pennies to make $1.98.

OUTFITS

MATHEMATICS STANDARDS ASSESSED

- Number operations and concepts
- Functions and algebra
- Statistics and probability
- Problem solving and mathematical reasoning
- Mathematical skills and tools, and
- Mathematical communication

DIRECTIONS TO THE STUDENT

Maria is going to visit her cousins for the weekend. She packs a pair of purple pants, a pair of jeans, and a pair of blue shorts. For shirts she takes a blue tee-shirt, a white tank top, a yellow blouse, and a green shirt. How many different outfits can she make?

A picture or table will help you to organize the information.

Write a description of how you figured out your answer.

MATHEMATICAL CONCEPT

This assessment task involves different combinations of a set of entities (in this case clothing). Each day Maria will wear one top, and one pair of either pants or shorts. Since she has four tops and three pants or shorts, her outfits may be listed and counted. The challenge for the student is to use a systematic approach that will ensure that all the possibilities have been considered.

SOLUTION

If the tops are assigned capitol letters (A, B, C, and D) and the pants or shorts are assigned numbers (1, 2, and 3), the outfits may be enumerated as A1, A2, A3, B1, B2, B3, C1, C2, C3, and D1, D2, D3. The total number of outfits is 4 x 3, or 12.

Many students will make a diagram to illustrate the situation, such as the following:

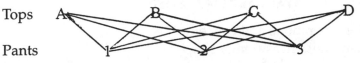

Tops

Pants

Alternatively, a student might determine that for each top, there are 3 possible outfits. Since there are four different tops, the total number of possible outfits is 4 x 3, or 12.

SCORING GUIDE

	Level One	Level Two	Level Three	Level Four
Organization of information	Information randomly presented.	Some attempt to organize the information; however the system is ineffective.	Information is organized in a fairly systematic manner.	Organization of information shows recognition of the patterns inherent in the situation.
Method of Solution	Either no method used or method completely inappropriate.	Appropriate method used, but either not fully executed or possibly based on rote application only.	Appropriate method used, and likely to yield correct answer.	Method used highly elegant and efficient, revealing comprehensive understanding.
Accuracy	Findings are wildly inaccurate.	Solution is only slightly inaccurate, resulting from errors in counting or multiplying.	Solution is accurate, with a total of 12 outfits for Maria.	In addition, the calculations demonstrate understanding of the .structure of the problem.
Description of procedure	Description either missing or reveals an approach to the problem only by trial and error.	Description reveals limited attempt to use a systematic approach, but not entirely successful.	Description adequately describes a systematic approach.	In addition, the explanation is efficient and clear, revealing complete understanding of how the problem can be solved mathematically.

PACKING TAPE

MATHEMATICS STANDARDS ASSESSED

- Number operations and concepts
- Geometry and measurement
- Problem solving and mathematical reasoning
- Mathematical skills and tools, and
- Mathematical communication

DIRECTIONS TO THE STUDENT

Your family is moving to a new house, and you are helping with packing your belongings. You and your family have decided that you will have 75 boxes to move; your mother has asked you to buy tape to close the boxes.

When you ask your mother how much tape to buy, she answers: "The boxes are 24" long, 18" wide, and 16" high. The boxes should be taped one time all the way around lengthwise. To make sure the boxes are secure, you will also need to put three strips of tape across the top."

How much tape will you need to do the job?

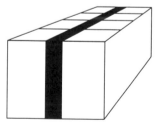

At the store, you find the following prices for tape:

50 yards @ $.99 per roll
100 yards @ $1.89 per roll
200 yards @ $3.29 per roll

How many rolls of each size will you buy, and what will be the total cost? Explain how you made your decision.

MATHEMATICAL CONCEPT

In completing this task, students must apply their understanding of the geometric concept of perimeter of a three dimensional object as well as make accurate calculations and convert between inches and yards.

This task is adapted from one developed by the Connecticut Department of Education.

SOLUTION

The distance around the box is 2 x 24" + 2 x 16" or 80". The amount of tape required for three straps across the top is 3 x 18" or 54". Therefore, the tape needed for each box is 80" + 54" or 134". For 75 boxes, 75 x 134" is required, or 1005". 1005" ÷ 36" is 279.17 yards. Therefore, one roll of 200 yards and one roll of 100 yards will be needed to tape all the boxes. The roll of 200 yards of tape will cost $3.29, while the roll of 100 yards will cost $1.89. Therefore, the total cost for the tape is $3.29 + $1.89 or $5.18.

SCORING GUIDE

	Level One	Level Two	Level Three	Level Four
Mathematical Accuracy	Many computational errors, leading to erroneous conclusions.	Some computational errors, but allowing largely for accurate conclusions.	Appropriate operation(s) selected; virtually no mathematical errors; with accurate conclusions.	In addition, all answers are shown in correct units.
Approach	Random and disorganized; no systematic approach.	Some system apparent in the approach; however, it is difficult to follow.	Systematic and organized approach, but not well presented.	Highly systematic and organized approach; neatly and clearly presented.
Explanation	Little or no explanation, or impossible to follow.	Explanation attempted, but difficult to understand.	Explanation fairly clear, but thinking process not always easy to follow.	Explanation very clear, and thinking process easy to follow.

PARTY PLANNING

MATHEMATICS STANDARDS ASSESSED

• Number operations and concepts,
• Problem solving and mathematical reasoning,
• Mathematical skills and tools, and
• Mathematical communication.

DIRECTIONS TO THE STUDENT

For your birthday you have invited five friends to your house for snacks and to watch a movie. Your mother has given you $13.00 to spend for the evening. You know that the movie rental is $4.00, and you can choose what to buy for the snacks. However, your mother has promised the other parents that **at least two** of the snacks will be **healthy foods.**

Decide what to buy for your party, using the prices below, making reasonable estimates of how much of each item your friends will want.

Make a list, with quantities, to show your mother, indicating how much it will cost, and using as much of the money as possible. Try to make your work as organized as possible, estimating how much your items will cost before you add them. You may use a calculator. The healthy foods are marked with an asterisk (*).

Cookies	$2.39
*Six-pack of yogurt	$1.90
Half-gallon of ice cream	$3.89
*Half-gallon of milk	$1.59
Six-pack of soda	$1.79
Large bag of chips	$1.79
*Box of six cheese pizzas	$4.89
*Bag of six oranges	$1.59
Microwave popcorn	$2.39
Big candy bar	$0.99

MATHEMATICAL CONCEPT

This task requires that students add numbers together in different combinations (using a calculator, if possible), and determine a plan. If students do not have access to a calculator, they will demonstrate their skill in adding numbers with re-grouping, or possibly in estimating.

This task is adapted from one developed by the Kentucky Department of Education.

SOLUTION

Many solutions are possible. Three possible solutions are: milk, oranges, either soda or chips, and candy bar for $8.35 + 4.00 for the movie = $12.35; yogurt, either milk or oranges, ice cream and candy bar for $8.37 + $4.00 movie = $12.37; pizzas, milk or oranges, and cookies for $8.87 + $4.00 movie = $12.87.

SCORING GUIDE

	Level One	Level Two	Level Three	Level Four
Mathematical Accuracy, and Use of Technology	Major computational errors, leading to highly erroneous conclusions.	Only minor errors, but allowing largely for accurate conclusions.	Virtually no mathematical errors; with accurate conclusions.	In addition, the work shows evidence of sophisticated use of technology.
Approach	Random and disorganized; no systematic approach.	Some system apparent in the approach; however, it is difficult to follow.	Systematic and organized approach, but not well presented.	Highly systematic and organized approach; neatly and clearly presented.

PARTY PRIZES

MATHEMATICS STANDARDS ASSESSED

- Number operations and concepts
- Problem solving and mathematical reasoning
- Mathematical skills and tools, and
- Mathematical communication

DIRECTIONS TO THE STUDENT

At a party six identical prizes were hidden. Anna and Beth both searched for them until all six were found.

In the table below, list all the different possible numbers of prizes that each girl could have found. One possibility has already been written into the table.

Number of Prizes found by Anna	Number of Prizes found by Beth
0	6

Explain why Beth could not have found exactly one more prize than Anna.

MATHEMATICAL CONCEPT

This task requires students to demonstrate two distinct but important concepts: creating an exhaustive list of two variables, and that the sum of two consecutive numbers cannot yield an even number.

This task is adapted from one developed by the New Standards Project.

SOLUTION

There are seven possible combinations for how Anna and Beth could have found the prizes:

Number of Prizes found by Anna	Number of Prizes found by Beth
0	6
1	5
2	4
3	3
4	2
5	1
6	0

Beth could not find one more prize than Anna since in that case one would have found an even number of prizes and the other an odd number of prizes, and the sum of an odd number and an even number is an odd number. However, since "six" is an even number, it must be the sum of either two odd numbers or two even numbers.

SCORING GUIDE

	Level One	Level Two	Level Three	Level Four
Mathematical Accuracy and Approach	Does not identify all the possible ways in which Beth and Anna could have found the prizes.	Identifies all the possible ways in which Beth and Anna could have found the prizes, but not in a systematic manner.	Identifies all the possible ways in which Beth and Anna could have found the prizes, in a moderately systematic manner.	Identifies all the possible ways in which Beth and Anna could have found the prizes, in a highly systematic manner.
Explanation	Either misunderstands the question or fails to recognize that Beth could not have found one more prize than Anna.	Attempts to answer the question but fails to recognize that Beth could not have found one more prize than Anna.	Explanation makes some mention of odd and even numbers, but is not clear.	Explanation makes explicit reference to the reason why Beth could not have found one more prize than Anna.

LEVEL ONE

Number of Prizes found by Anna	Number of Prizes found by Beth
0	6

Explain below why Beth could not have found exactly one more prize than Anna.

Beth would not find one more prize because she was not looking hard for the last prize and maybe she had a black eye and couldn't see right.

This response fails to identify all the possible combinations; furthermore, the student appears not to understand the question.

LEVEL ONE

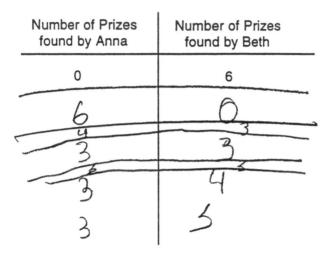

Number of Prizes found by Anna	Number of Prizes found by Beth
0	6
6	0
4	3
3	2
3	3
3	4
3	5

Explain below why Beth could not have found exactly one more prize than Anna.

She could have

LEVEL TWO

Number of Prizes found by Anna	Number of Prizes found by Beth
0	6
1	5
2	4
3	3
4	2
5	1
6	0

Explain below why Beth could not have found exactly one more prize than Anna.

There wasn't any more prizes left.

This response locates all the possible combinations, and in an organized manner. However, the explanation completely misses the mark.

LEVEL TWO

Number of Prizes found by Anna	Number of Prizes found by Beth
0	6
4	2
1	5
3	3
2	4
5	1
6	0

Explain below why Beth could not have found exactly one more prize than Anna.

Because there is only six prizes and Beth has all six that is why Beth could not have one more prize than Anna

---

This response locates all the possible combinations, although the approach is not an organized one. The explanation appears to miss the point of the question.

LEVEL THREE

Number of Prizes found by Anna	Number of Prizes found by Beth
0	6
1	5
2	4
3	3
4	2
5	1
6	0

Explain below why Beth could not have found exactly one more prize than Anna.

Because if she did, it would not equal six. Like, 6+5=11, 5+4=9, 4+3=7, 3+2=5, 2+1=3, and 1+0=1.

This response locates all the possible combinations, in an organized fashion. The student correctly concludes that Beth could not have found one more prize than Anna, and explains it by enumerating those possibilities. However, the student fails to recognize the reason behind that finding.

LEVEL THREE

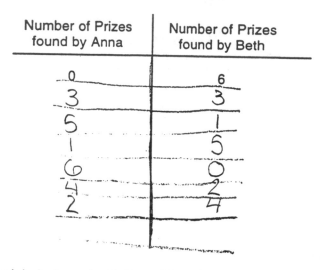

Number of Prizes found by Anna	Number of Prizes found by Beth
0	6
3	3
5	1
1	5
6	0
4	2
2	4

Explain below why Beth could not have found exactly one more prize than Anna.

Beth can't because 6 is an even number & it can be split up lots of ways.

This response locates all the possible combinations, in an organized fashion. The student correctly concludes that Beth could not have found one more prize than Anna, and recognizes that the reason has something to do with odd and even numbers. However, the reason is not clearly stated, and is probably not completely understood.

LEVEL FOUR

Number of Prizes found by Anna	Number of Prizes found by Beth
0	6
1	5
2	4
3	3
4	2
5	1
6	0

Explain below why Beth could not have found exactly one more prize than Anna.

Beth couldn't get one more prize because you would always have only an even number between the two numbers

This response locates all the possible combinations, in an organized fashion, and the student correctly concludes that Beth could not have found one more prize than Anna. The reason given is unusual, but accurate. By stating that the difference between the two numbers is an even number, the student is saying, indirectly, that the difference cannot be "1."

LEVEL FOUR

Number of Prizes found by Anna	Number of Prizes found by Beth
0	6
6	0
3	3
4	2
2	4
1	5
5	1

Explain below why Beth could not have found exactly one more prize than Anna.

Beth can't find one more than Anna because then it would be odd + even and odd+even is an odd number but 6 is a even number so if you had exactly one more the sum would be an odd number.

This response locates all the possible combinations, in an organized fashion. The student correctly concludes that Beth could not have found one more prize than Anna, and provides an accurate and conventional reason. While not neatly presented, the answer is complete and accurate.

PEANUTS

MATHEMATICS STANDARDS ASSESSED

- Number operations and concepts
- Problem solving and mathematical reasoning
- Mathematical skills and tools, and
- Mathematical communication.

DIRECTIONS TO THE STUDENT

The students in Ms. Hartman's class bought some peanuts that come in small bags. Each student in the class reported how many peanuts were in his or her bag. Here are the results:

NUMBER OF PEANUTS IN A BAG

14   17   15   16   16   18   21   13   15   14   15

15   16   17   17   19   17   16   19   15   19

If someone asked you "About how many peanuts are in a bag?" what would you say? How many possible answers are there? Explain the reasons for your answer or answers.

MATHEMATICAL CONCEPT

In this task students must calculate the average of a group of numbers. They can calculate the mean, the median, or the mode; any choice should be justified.

This task is slightly adapted from one developed by the Oregon Department of Education.

SOLUTION

The number of peanuts in the bags may be shown as follows:

Number of Peanuts in a Bag	Number of Bags
13	1
14	2
15	5
16	4
17	4
18	1
19	3
20	0
21	1

The mean number of peanuts in each bag is 16.38 (344 ÷ 21 = 16.38.) The median is slightly greater than 16 (there are 8 data points below 16 and 9 points above 16.) On the other hand, there are 5 bags with 15 peanuts; therefore, 15 is the mode.

SCORING GUIDE

	Level One	Level Two	Level Three	Level Four
Mathematical Accuracy	No attempt to calculate the mean, the median, or the mode.	May have minor errors in calculating the mean, median, or mode. No indication of awareness of the median or the mode.	Correct calculation of the mean number of peanuts; indication of awareness of the median and/or the mode.	Correct calculation of the mean, the median, and the mode of the number of peanuts in a bag.
Approach	Random and disorganized; no systematic approach.	Some system apparent in the approach; for example a frequency chart or graph; however, it is difficult to follow.	Systematic and organized approach, for example a frequency chart or graph; but not well presented.	Highly systematic and organized approach; neatly and clearly presented.
Explanation	Little or no explanation, or impossible to follow.	Explanation attempted, but difficult to understand.	Explanation fairly clear, but thinking process not always easy to follow..	Explanation very clear, and thinking process easy to follow.

LEVEL ONE

Number of Peanuts in a Bag

14 17 15 16 16 18 21 23 15 14 15
15 16 17 17 19 17 16 19 15 19

If someone asked you "About how many peanuts are in a bag?" what would you say? How many possible answers are there? Explain the reasons for your answer or answers.

I think there are (9) different ansers. Even though there are 21 bags there are like three, 17s and so on. There are only (9) numbers not counting the pairs.

This response appears to have been answering a different question, such as "how many different numbers are represented by the peanuts in the bags?" The response simply does not answer the question as asked.

LEVEL ONE

There
could be eany aiswer, you neler now how meany
pehuts in a sag. Thfe coula be a 1,000
000 200 308 mabe 900, There ar ncler the Same
amont,

This response misses the point of the question and argues that there could be any number of peanuts in the bag. Since there is never the same amount of peanuts, it could be any number, 100, 200, 300, or even 900. This student appears to have a weak number sense, particularly of large numbers.

LEVEL TWO

The ahsewen is 16 because
I found the average and it
was 16

This response is a clear "2," finding the mean, but with no
mention of other possible ways of answering the question.

LEVEL TWO

No 15
because there are the most 15's

This student notes that "there are more "15's" than any other number, so that is the answer to the question. The student has identified the mode but has not mentioned the possibility of other ways of answering the question.

LEVEL THREE

Number of Peanuts in a Bag

14   17   15   16   16   18   21   13   15   14   15
  15   16   17   17   19   17   16   19   15   19

If someone asked you "About how many peanuts are in a bag?" what would you say? How many possible answers are there? Explain the reasons for your answer or answers.

There are about 16-8 peanuts

The possible ways to find out is
4. The ways are Mode, Mean, Median, and Range

This response correctly calculates the mean, but fails to recognize that the "remainder 8" cannot be part of the answer. The response also mentions the mode, median and range, suggesting that these concepts would also yield answers.

LEVEL THREE

about 16 because I found the average.
a couple of other possible anwsers
are: 15, or 17 because the appear a?
lot above,

This response correctly identifies 16 as the average number of peanuts in the bags. The student also suggests that there are other possible answers, including 15 since these numbers appear a lot above.

LEVEL FOUR

17 or 16, because if you add all of them up and divide by 21 you get 16. If you just look at the numbers, there are as much 17's as 16's. Also 15, because there more 15's then any other number.

This response is a low 4. The student clearly understands that there are different ways to think about the question, and correctly identifies two of them (the mean and the mode.) It is not absolutely clear, however, that the student understands the distinction between the mean and the median.

LEVEL FOUR

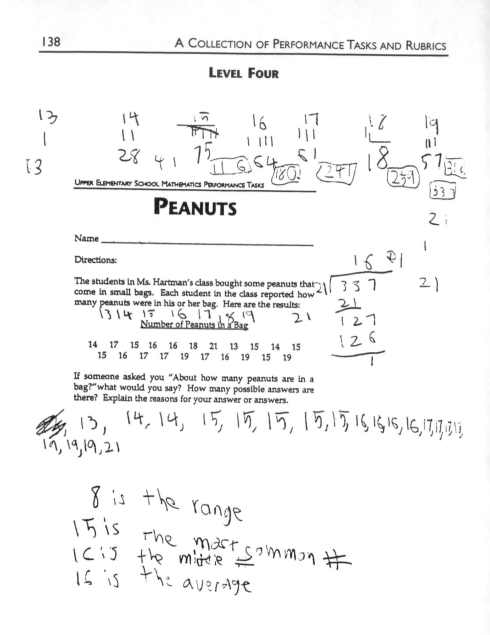

UPPER ELEMENTARY SCHOOL MATHEMATICS PERFORMANCE TASKS

PEANUTS

Name _____

Directions:

The students in Ms. Hartman's class bought some peanuts that come in small bags. Each student in the class reported how many peanuts were in his or her bag. Here are the results:

Number of Peanuts in a Bag

14	17	15	16	16	18	21	13	15	14	15
15	16	17	17	19	17	16	19	15	19	

If someone asked you "About how many peanuts are in a bag?" what would you say? How many possible answers are there? Explain the reasons for your answer or answers.

13, 14, 14, 15, 15, 15, 15, 15, 16, 16, 16, 16, 17, 17, 17, 19, 19, 19, 21

8 is the range
15 is the most common #
16 is the middle common #
16 is the average

This response clearly identifies the mean, median, and mode by their properties, indicating good understanding of the concepts.

PET SURVEY

MATHEMATICS STANDARDS ASSESSED

- Problem solving and mathematical reasoning
- Statistics and probability
- Mathematical skills and tools, and
- Mathematical communication

DIRECTIONS TO THE STUDENT

Which pets do you think are most popular with the families of students in your school? In this problem you will take a survey of students in one class, and compare your results with those of classmates who have surveyed students in another class.

To do this task, you should:

- design a questionnaire to use with students in another class, to find out how many and what types of pets they have at home
- survey all the students in the other class
- summarize your results
- make a graph of your findings
- compare your graph with at least one classmate, and
- write a comparison of the information in your graph with that of your classmate

Note to the teacher: arrangements will have to be made for students to conduct their surveys. While students may be able to get their information during recess, it is more likely that they will have to visit the class during school hours.

MATHEMATICAL CONCEPT

This task engages students in data collection, analysis, and interpretation. Depending on how different the pets are in the different classes, they may also deal with issues of the representative nature of their data.

SOLUTION

There are, of course, many possible answers to this task, depending on what pets students have at home. But a successful response will include a well-designed survey instrument, data clearly organized by reasonable categories, accurate conclusions, and valid comparisons made with the pets in another class.

SCORING GUIDE

	Level One	Level Two	Level Three	Level Four
Design of Survey Instrument	Questions very limited; will not serve to obtain necessary information about pets.	Questions will elicit almost all information about pets required for the task.	Questions will elicit all information about pets required	In addition, questions asked in a manner to ease later data analysis.
Analysis of Data	Data poorly organized; hard to read and interpret.	Data organization is uneven.	Data organized but difficult to use for making a graph.	Data well organized and neatly presented.
Quality of Graph	Graph seriously flawed: inappropriate type, inaccurate, or error in execution.	Graph has one serious error	Graph is appropriate to the data, and is accurate.	In addition, the graph is well presented, with all details well executed.
Comparison With Classmate's Graph	Comparison either absent or cites irrelevant details.	Minor errors in the interpretation of findings.	Interpretation of data essentially accurate; data support findings.	In addition, the findings are presented in an imaginative manner.

PIECES OF PIZZA

MATHEMATICS STANDARDS ASSESSED

- Number operations and concepts
- Geometry and measurement
- Problem solving and mathematical reasoning
- Mathematical skills and tools, and
- Mathematical communication.

DIRECTIONS TO THE STUDENT

Jose ate 1/2 of a pizza. Ella ate 1/2 of another pizza. Jose said that he ate more pie than Ella did, but she said they both ate the same amount. Who do you think is right? Is it possible that neither Jose nor Ella is correct? Use drawings or pictures and words to explain your answer.

MATHEMATICAL CONCEPT

In this task, students must consider the idea of a fraction of a shape, and consider the possibility that the pies might be different sizes.

This task is adapted from one developed by the New Standards Project.

SOLUTION

Only if the pies are the same size is Ella correct. If the pies are different sizes, and if Jose's pie is larger, then Jose is correct. It Ella's pie is larger, then neither one is correct since Ella ate more pie. Students' drawings and explanations should make it clear that they understand the relationship between the size of the pies and the size of one-half the pie.

SCORING GUIDE

	Level One	Level Two	Level Three	Level Four
Drawing	Drawing demonstrates little understanding of the problem	Drawing reflects limited understanding of the problem.	Drawing reflects complete understanding of the problem.	In addition, the drawing is done to scale and neatly presented.
Explanation	Explanation muddled or reflects lack of understanding of the value of fractions of different sizes of pie.	Explanation unclear as to the relationship between the size of pie and the fraction eaten.	Explanation reveals moderate understanding of the relationship between size of pie and fraction.	Explanation reveals extended understanding of the relationship between size of pie and fraction.

LEVEL ONE

He could have cut his half of pizza this way / she could of cut hers this wa ——.

Jose   Ella

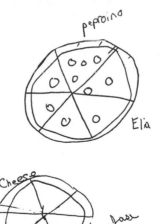

This response demonstrates little understanding of the problem. Apparently the student believes that cutting the pizza horizontally or vertically causes the amount of pizza to vary.

peproino

Ella

Cheese

Jose

This response does not answer the question at all. The response consists only of two drawings of pizza, one labeled "cheese" and the other labeled "peproino." The issue of the amount of pizza eaten by Ella and Jose is not addressed at all.

Level Two

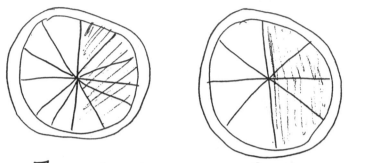

The pizza pie of Jose could of been sliced different than Ellas, OR one could of gotten a midium and a large.

The first part of this response appears to confuse the manner in which a pizza is sliced with the amount of pie to be eaten. The second half of the response, on the other hand, offers a limited, but correct, response. However, it is presented almost as an afterthought. The student may have become aware of the correct response while answering the questions initially.

LEVEL TWO

Jose ate 8 slices

Ella ate 4 slices

But they still ate half of a pizza

This response indicates that the student understands that Jose could have been correct. However, the student confuses the number of pieces eaten with the amount of pizza.

JOSe Ralf

Ella

half

The drawing in this response indicates an understanding of the relationship between the size of the pizza and the amount eaten. However, since there is no explanation, it is not certain that the student understands the concept.

LEVEL THREE

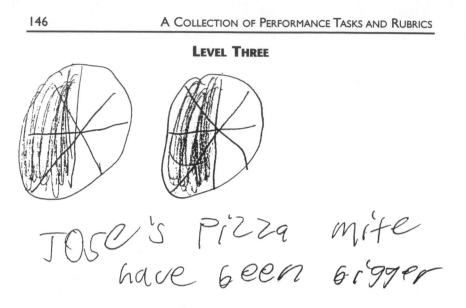

Jose's pizza mite have been brigger

This response is a weak 3, in that the drawing is unclear. However, the explanation indicates that the student understands that Jose could have eaten more pizza by eating one-half of a larger pizza than Ella's.

Jose have eaten half of a large pizza and Ella eaten half of a small pizza and that means Jose could of eaten more, but still eaten half.

This response is a weak 3 in that it does not include a drawing at all. However, since the explanation is very clear, the student has demonstrated understanding of the relationship between the amount of pizza eaten and the size of the pizza.

LEVEL FOUR

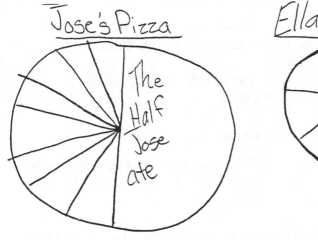

Jose's Pizza

Ella's Pizza

The Half Jose ate

The Half Ella ate

Jose could be right if he ate a larger pizza than Ella.

This response is a clear "four" although it would be stronger with a neater drawing. However, both through the drawing and the explanation the student indicates complete understanding of the problem and its solution.

PIZZA CHOICES

MATHEMATICS STANDARDS ASSESSED

• Number operations and concepts
• Problem solving and mathematical reasoning
• Statistics and probability
• Mathematical skills and tools, and
• Mathematical communication

DIRECTIONS TO THE STUDENT

The director of your school cafeteria has decided to offer pizza on Fridays, but is not sure what kind to provide. Your class has been asked to help decide.

1. Devise a method to determine what kind of pizza students in another class in the school prefer. Interview or survey students in that class.

2. Summarize, using both words and a graph, the information you have collected.

3. Write a letter to the cafeteria manager, explaining whether you think your survey can serve as the basis for deciding the school's Friday lunch menu.

MATHEMATICAL CONCEPT

In this task, students must develop a survey or interview instrument that enables students to indicate their pizza preferences, summarize and graph the results, and determine whether their results are representative of the school as a whole.

This task is adapted from one developed by the California Department of Education.

SOLUTION

There are many possible solutions to this task, depending, of course, on the actual pizza preferences of students. But all successful solutions will contain a well-designed survey instrument or interview form, a way to summarize the information, a graph, and a clear explanation of the nature of the results.

SCORING GUIDE

	Level One	Level Two	Level Three	Level Four
Design of Survey Instrument	Questions very limited; will not serve to obtain necessary information about pizza preferences.	Questions will elicit almost all information about pizza preferences required for the task.	Questions will elicit all information about pizza preferences required	In addition, questions asked in a manner to ease later data analysis.
Analysis of Data	Data poorly organized; hard to read and interpret.	Data organization is uneven.	Data organized but difficult to use for making a graph.	Data well organized and neatly presented.
Quality of Graph	Graph seriously flawed: inappropriate type, inaccurate, or error in execution.	Graph has one serious error	Graph is appropriate to the data, and is accurate.	In addition, the graph is well presented, with all details well executed.
Letter to the Cafeteria Manager	Ideas are not accurately summarized; a manager could not act on the findings.	Letter summarizes the survey findings, but difficult to follow.	Letter accurately and clearly summarizes the survey findings.	In addition, the findings are presented in an imaginative manner.

SALE PRICE

MATHEMATICS STANDARDS ASSESSED

• Number operations and concepts
• Problem solving and mathematical reasoning
• Statistics and probability
• Mathematical skills and tools, and
• Mathematical communication

DIRECTIONS TO THE STUDENT

Brian's bicycle shop had 48 water bottles for sale, but since winter was coming he wanted to sell as many as he could. On Monday, Brian marked the water bottles down to $5.00 each and sold 1/2 of them. On Tuesday, he marked the remaining bottles down to $4.00 each and sold 1/2 of what was left. On Wednesday, he marked the remaining bottles down to $3.00 and sold 1/3 of the remaining bottles. On Thursday Brian marked the remaining bottles down to $2.00 and sold them all.

If Brian paid $4.00 each for the bottles, how much money did he gain or lose in selling these bottles? Explain your reasons.

MATHEMATICAL CONCEPT

In this task students must apply concepts of unit fractions to a practical situation, and must perform calculations accurately.

This task is adapted from one developed by the Oregon Department of Education.

SOLUTION

This problem, unlike many performance assessments, has a single correct answer. On Monday, when Brian sold 1/2 the water bottles for $5.00, he received $120 (24 x $5.). On Tuesday, he received $48 (12 x $4.). On Wednesday he received $12 (4 x $3.), and on Thursday he received $6. (8 x $2.). In total, he realized

$196 from the sale of the water bottles over the four days ($120. + $48. + $12. + $16.) However, if Brian paid $4.00 for each bottle, he spent $192.00 on them (48 x $4.00). Therefore, his profit on the sale of the water bottles is $4.00.

SCORING GUIDE

	Level One	Level Two	Level Three	Level Four
Mathematical Accuracy	Many computational errors, leading to wildly erroneous conclusions.	Some computational errors, but allowing largely for accurate conclusions.	Virtually no mathematical errors; with accurate conclusions.	Completely accurate computation, allowing for accurate conclusions.
Approach	Random and disorganized; no systematic approach.	Some system apparent in the approach; however, it is difficult to follow.	Systematic and organized approach, but not well presented.	Highly systematic and organized approach; neatly and clearly presented.
Explanation	Little or no explanation, or impossible to follow.	Explanation attempted, but difficult to understand.	Explanation fairly clear, but thinking process not always easy to follow.	Explanation very clear, and thinking process easy to follow.

SCHOOL PLAY

MATHEMATICS STANDARDS ASSESSED

- Number operations and concepts
- Problem solving and mathematical reasoning
- Mathematical skills and tools, and
- Mathematical communication.

DIRECTIONS TO THE STUDENT

Tickets to the school play cost $1.00 for students and $2.00 for adults.

1. If $125 was collected, how many adults and how many students could have attended the play? How many different possible answers are there to this question? Find as many as you can.

2. If programs for the play cost $.50 to produce, how much profit would the school make with different combinations of students and adults attending the play? If the school wanted to make as much profit as possible, would it encourage students or adults to attend the play?

3. Write a letter to the play's manager explaining how you think profits can be made as large as possible.

MATHEMATICAL CONCEPT

In this task, students must apply elementary computational skills to a realistic situation, dealing with two separate variables. They must recognize that since adults pay twice as much as students, but their programs cost the same to produce, profits are larger when as many adults as possible attend the play.

SOLUTION

There are many combinations of students and adults that could have attended the play such that the number of students + 2 x (number of adults) = $125. If programs cost $.50 to print, possible answers are:

Number of Students	Number of Adults	Total Number	Total Profit
15	55	70	$90
35	45	80	$85
55	35	90	$80
75	25	100	$75
95	15	110	$70
115	5	120	$65

Clearly, the more adults and the fewer students attending the play, the greater the profits after the printing of the programs is paid for.

SCORING GUIDE

	Level One	Level Two	Level Three	Level Four
Mathematical Accuracy	Inappropriate operation(s) selected, and/or many errors, leading to wildly erroneous conclusions.	Mixture of appropriate and inappropriate operation(s); some errors, but allowing largely for accurate conclusions.	Appropriate operation(s) selected; virtually no mathematical errors; with accurate conclusions.	In addition, the work shows evidence of advanced planning.
Approach	Random and disorganized; no systematic approach.	Some system apparent in the approach; however, it is difficult to follow.	Systematic and organized approach, but not well presented.	Highly systematic and organized approach; neatly and clearly presented.
Explanation	Little or no explanation, or impossible to follow.	Explanation attempted, but difficult to understand.	Explanation fairly clear, but thinking process not always easy to follow.	Explanation very clear, and thinking process easy to follow.

School Supplies

Mathematics Standards Assessed

- Number operations and concepts
- Problem solving and mathematical reasoning
- Mathematical skills and tools, and
- Mathematical communication

Directions To The Student

It is almost the end of summer vacation, and time to buy school supplies. You have ads from two different stores showing their prices for different school items. Your cousin has given you $20 to spend, and wants you to find the best prices on the things you need.

School Supplies Needed

> 4 folders
> calculator
> lined paper (pack of 200 sheets)
> ruler (with both standard and metric units)
> set of 24 felt tipped pens
> backpack
> 10 pencils

1. Determine the cheapest source for each of the items on the list of school supplies. Make a list that will tell you which items to buy from each store. How much will you have to spend, and how much of the $20.00 will you have left over?

2. If you have time to go to only one store, which store would give you best value? What would be the cost of all the items on the list, and how much change would you receive from the $20.00?

Is it worth the trouble to go to both stores? Write a brief note to your cousin explaining why you think it is (or is not) worth the trouble to go to both.

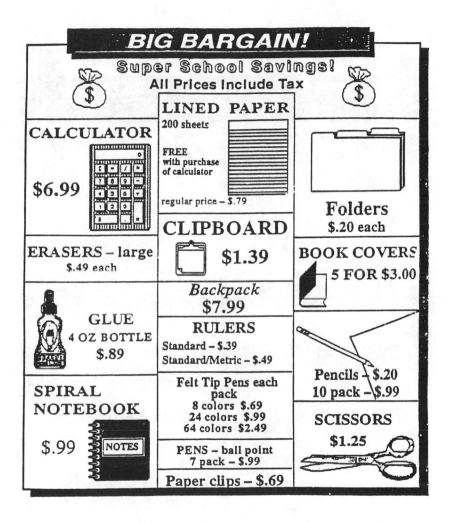

BIG BARGAIN!

Super School Savings!

All Prices Include Tax

CALCULATOR

$6.99

LINED PAPER

200 sheets

FREE
with purchase
of calculator

regular price – $.79

CLIPBOARD   **$1.39**

Folders
$.20 each

ERASERS – large
$.49 each

BOOK COVERS
5 FOR $3.00

GLUE
4 OZ BOTTLE
$.89

Backpack
$7.99

RULERS
Standard – $.39
Standard/Metric – $.49

Pencils – $.20
10 pack – $.99

**SPIRAL
NOTEBOOK**

$.99   NOTES

Felt Tip Pens each
pack
8 colors $.69
24 colors $.99
64 colors $2.49

PENS – ball point
7 pack – $.99

Paper clips – $.69

SCISSORS
$1.25

MATHEMATICAL CONCEPT

In this task requires that students use a systematic approach to organizing a lot of information. They apply simple computational skills to make a judgment about best value for money.

This task is adapted from one developed by New Standards™.

SOLUTION

The prices for the required items from "Big Bargain" and "Super Value" are listed below:

	Big Bargain	Super Value
4 folders	.80	1.00
calculator	6.99	4.00
lined paper (200 sheets)	.79	.79
	(free with calculator)	
ruler	.49	.69
pens	.99	.78
pencils	.99	1.98
backpack	7.99	9.99
Total	18.25	19.23
Change from $20.00	1.75	.77

On the other hand, if each item is purchased at the cheapest source, the list for each store would be as follows:

Big Bargain	Super Value
folders ($.80)	calculator ($4.00)
ruler ($.49)	pens ($.78)
pencils ($.99)	
backpack ($7.99)	

In addition, the lined paper can be purchased at either store, since the price is the same. Therefore, if the paper is purchased at Big Bargain, the total cost at that store is $11.06 while the total at Super Value is $4.78 for a grand total of $15.84, with $4.16 remaining from the $20.00. Whether students believe it is worth the trouble to go to both stores will reflect the value they place on the money saved ($3.39).

SCORING GUIDE

	Level One	Level Two	Level Three	Level Four
Mathematical Accuracy	Inappropriate operation(s) selected, and/or many errors, leading to wildly erroneous conclusions.	Mixture of appropriate and inappropriate operation(s); some errors, but allowing largely for accurate conclusions.	Appropriate operation(s) selected; virtually no mathematical errors; with accurate conclusions.	In addition, the work shows evidence of advanced planning.
Approach	Random and disorganized; no systematic approach.	Some system apparent in the approach; however, it is difficult to follow	Systematic and organized approach, but not well presented.	Highly systematic and organized approach; neatly and clearly presented.
Explanation	Little or no explanation, or impossible to follow.	Explanation attempted, but difficult to understand.	Explanation fairly clear, but thinking process not always easy to follow.	Explanation very clear, and thinking process easy to follow.

SCIENCE FAIR

MATHEMATICS STANDARDS ASSESSED

- Number operations and concepts
- Geometry and measurement
- Problem solving and mathematical reasoning, and
- Mathematical communication

DIRECTIONS TO THE STUDENT

Three elementary schools are planning a science fair, which will be held in a multi-purpose room of one of the schools. Space in the multi-purpose room will be allocated to each school according to the number of students in the school: the more students, the more space given to that school.

Jackson School has about 500 students. Kennedy School has about 200 students. Martin Luther King School has about 300 students.

The rectangle below represents the multi-purpose room where the science fair will he held. Show the amount of space each school should get based on each school's population. Label each section J for Jackson School, K for Kennedy School, and M for Martin Luther King School.

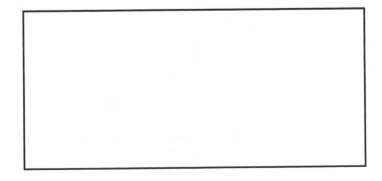

Write a description of how you decided to divide the space. How do you know it is fair?

MATHEMATICAL CONCEPT

This task involves at least an intuitive application of concepts of proportionality and percent, in that students must apportion the space in the multi-purpose room according to the populations of the different schools. While students are not required to formally convert fractions into percents, they must demonstrate at least a conceptual understanding of these ideas.

This task is adapted from one developed by the New Standards Project.

SOLUTION

A successful solution to this problem will recognize that Jackson School students should have roughly half the space, with Kennedy School and Martin Luther King School splitting the remaining half in the ratio of two-fifths to three-fifths. Actual drawings, of course, will vary, but all correct solutions will share these characteristics. A possible correct solution is shown below.

SCORING GUIDE

	Level One	Level Two	Level Three	Level Four
Accuracy	Drawing appears random with no apparent recognition of the proportion of total students represented by the different schools.	Drawing is rough, but demonstrates some recognition of the proportion of total students represented by the different schools.	Drawing demonstrates clear recognition of the proportion of total students represented by the different schools.	In addition, the work is very neatly presented.
Explanation	Little or no explanation, or impossible to follow. No mention of the proportions of students in the different schools.	Explanation attempted, but difficult to understand. Only muddled reference to the proportions of students in the different schools.	Explanation provides explicit reference to the proportions of students in the different schools.	Explanation provides explicit reference to the proportions of students in the different schools and links it to the share of space for the science fair.

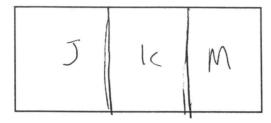

Write a description of how you decided to divide the space.
How do you know it is fair?

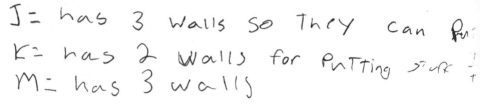

J = has 3 walls so They can pu
K = has 2 walls for PuTTing stuff
M = has 3 walls

This response makes no mention of the number of students in
the different schools, and suggests that the important consideration for a science fair is the amount of wall space. It is possible that this student has had no experience with science fairs.

Level Two

Write a description of how you decided to divide the space.
How do you know it is fair?

Jackson school, has the most
space, because it has the most
students, then MLK school, then
Kennedy school

This response reflects only the most global sense of the amount
of space that should be allocated to each school, referring to the
fact that Jackson has the "most" number of students, MLK the
next most, and Kennedy the least. The drawing does not provide any more specific indication of the student's understanding of the proportional share of each school of the total number
of students.

LEVEL TWO

Write a description of how you decided to divide the space.
How do you know it is fair?

If you add all of the numbers together they equal 1000 Half of 1000 is 500 Then you know that you have just make the other half into a big pice and a little pice.

This response indicates understanding that the students at Jackson should have one-half the space, since half the students attend Jackson. However, the student then estimates the amount of space to be allocated to the other two schools.

LEVEL THREE

Jackson	MLK	Kennedy

Write a description of how you decided to divide the space.
How do you know it is fair? I gave Jackson 1/2 because all together there are 1,000 students + 500 in Jackson. I gave MLK 2/3 of the empty half + Kennedy 1/3 of the empty half.

This response recognizes that the space allocated to Jackson school should consist of one-half the total amount. However, in calculating the space for the other two schools, the student suggests one-third and two-thirds of the remaining space, which would give the King School twice the space of Kennedy School.

LEVEL THREE

Write a description of how you decided to divide the space.
How do you know it is fair?

The whole is 1000 people
500 is ½ 300 is about ⅜ and 200
is ¼

This response also recognizes that the space allocated to
Jackson school should consist of one-half the total amount.
However, the fractions provided for the other two schools are
muddled.

LEVEL FOUR

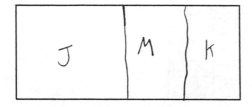

Write a description of how you decided to divide the space.
How do you know it is fair? All toghethet there are 1,000 students
So half goes to Jackson School, 1/5 goes to Kenedy
School, and a little more then 1/5 goes to Martin Luther
King School.

This response represents a low four. It correctly states that
Jackson School should have one-half the space and that the
Kennedy School should have one-fifth. However, the student
is unsure of the fraction that should be allocated to the King
School.

LEVEL FOUR

Write a description of how you decided to divide the space.
How do you know it is fair?

First I divided the rectangle into 10th
Then I gave Kennedy $\frac{2}{10}$ because they have 200
students. I gave Martin Luther King school $\frac{3}{10}$
because they have 300 students and then I gave

Jackson school $\frac{5}{10}$ because they have 500 stud.
Its fair because I divided into 8 tenths
and then gave each school a number of
tenths according to their number of students

This response is a solid four, demonstrating clear understanding of the situation and a good explanation. The student followed an interesting approach, and calculated the number of tenths needed by the students from each school.

SPINNING ADVANTAGE

MATHEMATICS STANDARDS ASSESSED

- Number operations and concepts
- Geometry and measurement
- Problem solving and mathematical reasoning
- Statistics and probability, and
- Mathematical communication

DIRECTIONS TO THE STUDENT

You and a friend are playing a game, using the spinner below. One of you gets a point every time the spinner lands on an odd number; the other gets a point when it lands on an even number. The first person to reach 21 points wins the game. Would you prefer to get the point for the odd or even numbers? Why? Explain why you think that would be better.

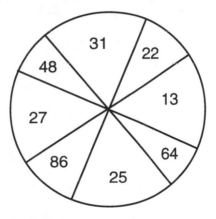

MATHEMATICAL CONCEPT

This task requires students to apply certain elementary notions of probability and to integrate those concepts with an understanding of odd and even numbers.

This task is adapted from one developed by the New Standards Project

SOLUTION

It is obvious from simply looking at the spinner that the odd numbers cover a larger area of the spinner than do the even numbers. Therefore, if the spinner is balanced, it is preferable to have the odd numbers.

SCORING GUIDE

	Level One	Level Two	Level Three	Level Four
Conceptual Understanding	Response demonstrates little or no understanding of either even and odd numbers or probability.	Response demonstrates only limited understanding of either even and odd numbers or probability.	Response demonstrates moderate understanding of both even and odd numbers and probability.	Response demonstrates comprehensive understanding of both even and odd numbers and probability.
Explanation	Little or no explanation, or impossible to follow.	Explanation attempted, but difficult to understand.	Explanation fairly clear, but thinking process not always easy to follow.	Explanation very clear, and thinking process easy to follow.

VENDING VALUE

MATHEMATICS STANDARDS ASSESSED

- Number operations and concepts
- Problem solving and mathematical reasoning
- Statistics and probability
- Mathematical skills and tools, and
- Mathematical communication

DIRECTIONS TO THE STUDENT

Carlos wants to buy a 75-cent snack from a vending machine. The machine accepts only nickels, dimes, and quarters. Carlos has 7 nickels, 5 dimes, and 2 quarters.

1. What are all the possible ways that Carlos could pay for the snack? You may use words or pictures.

2. Which of your ways would use the fewest number of coins? Explain why this is so.

MATHEMATICAL CONCEPT

This task requires students to devise a strategy for identifying all the possible combinations of coins for a particular sum. Such a strategy, in order to locate them all, must be organized and systematic.

This task is adapted from one developed by the California Department of Education.

SOLUTION

There are nine possible ways to make 75 cents from the coins Carlos has:

Number of Coins	Quarters	Dimes	Nickels
5	2	2	1
6	2	1	3
6	1	5	0
7	2	0	5
7	1	4	2
8	1	3	4
8	1	2	6
10	0	5	5
11	0	4	7

Clearly, the most "efficient" solutions use the largest possible number of the largest denomination coins.

SCORING GUIDE

	Level One	Level Two	Level Three	Level Four
Mathematical Accuracy and Approach	Random and disorganized; no systematic approach; inaccurate conclusions.	Some system apparent in the approach, but not all combinations found; only minor errors, allowing largely for accurate conclusions.	Systematic approach used, and most combinations found. Accurate conclusions regarding the optimal combination of coins.	Highly systematic and organized approach, with all combinations found. Correct conclusions made about the most efficient combination of coins; neatly and clearly presented.
Explanation	Little or no explanation, or impossible to follow.	Explanation attempted, but difficult to understand; unclear whether the principle of using the coins of the largest denomination is understood.	Explanation fairly clear, but thinking process not always easy to follow. Response indicated understanding of the principle of using the coins of the largest denomination.	Explanation very clear, and thinking process easy to follow, with explicit mention of the principle of using the coins of the largest denomination.

WHEELS

MATHEMATICS STANDARDS ASSESSED

- Number operations and concepts
- Problem solving and mathematical reasoning
- Statistics and probability
- Mathematical skills and tools, and
- Mathematical communication

DIRECTIONS TO THE STUDENT

Toni and her friends take their tricycles and wagons to the playground. If Toni counted 29 wheels, how many tricycles and how many wagons were at the playground?

Is there another possible combination of wagons and tricycles? Show how you got your answers.

MATHEMATICAL CONCEPT

This task requires that students make different combinations of 3's and 4's and add them together. In order to find both possible combinations, they must develop a systematic approach and maintain flexibility.

This task is adapted from one developed by the New Standards Project.

SOLUTION

There are two possible combinations of wagons and tricycles that could produce 29 wheels: 3 tricycles and 5 wagons, and 7 tricycles and 2 wagons.

SCORING GUIDE

	Level One	Level Two	Level Three	Level Four
Mathematical Accuracy	Does not find even one correct combination of wheels, or does not understand the problem.	Finds one correct combination of wheels.	Finds both correct combinations of wheels.	Finds both correct combinations of wheels.
Approach	Random and disorganized; no system apparent in the approach.	Hints of a systematic approach are evident; but may revert to trial and error.	Some system apparent in the approach; however, it is not entirely successful..	Uses a systematic and organized approach; neatly and clearly presented.

LEVEL ONE

There is 3 wagons and 4 tricycles.

This responses offers only one answer to the problem, which is incorrect.

$$+\begin{array}{r}11\\18\\\hline 29\end{array}$$

They had 11 tricycles and 18 wagons

This student appears to have confused the number of wheels with the number of vehicles. Using this approach, there would have been many more possible combinations, which the student did not recognize.

LEVEL TWO

$$\begin{array}{r} 3 \\ 3 \\ + 3 \\ \hline 9 \end{array}$$

$$\begin{array}{r} 9 \\ 4 \\ 4 \\ 4 \\ 4 \\ \hline 20 \\ + 9 \\ \hline 29 \end{array}$$

5 wagons
3 tricycles

In this response the student identified one correct solution to the problem, but did not use a systematic approach to finding more.

There were 7 tricycles and 2 wagons.
No, there is not another possible combination of wagons and tricycles.

$$\begin{array}{r} 3 \text{ wheels} \\ \times 7 \\ \hline 21 \text{ wheels} \end{array}$$

$$\begin{array}{r} 4 \text{ wheels} \\ \times 2 \\ \hline 8 \text{ wheels} \end{array}$$

$$\begin{array}{r} 21 \text{ wheels} \\ + 8 \text{ wheels} \\ \hline 29 \text{ wheels} \end{array}$$

This response is better explained and represents slightly better thinking than the answer above; however, it also identifies only one correct answer to the question.

LEVEL THREE

$3 \times 0 = 0$

$3 \times 1 = 3$

$3 \times 2 = 6$

$3 \times 3 = 9$

$3 \times 4 = 12$

$3 \times 5 = 15$

$3 \times 6 = 18$

$3 \times 7 = 21$

$3 \times 8 = 24$

$3 \times 9 = 27$

$4 \times 0 = 0$

$4 \times 1 = 4$

$4 \times 2 = 8$

$4 \times 3 = 12$

$4 \times 4 = 16$

$4 \times 5 = 20$

$4 \times 6 = 24$

$4 \times 7 = 28$

This response is a weak "3" because it does not identify even a single correct answer to the question. However, the student presents a highly organized approach, and with an additional step could easily have found both correct answers. This student may have simply run out of time to finish the task.

LEVEL THREE

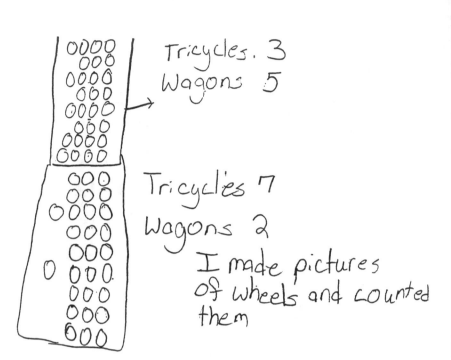

Tricycles. 3
Wagons 5

Tricycles 7
Wagons 2

I made pictures
of wheels and counted
them

This response correctly identifies both answers to the question, and presents what appears to be a hint of a systematic approach. However, this student's thinking was most likely a refinement of trial and error rather than a true system.

LEVEL FOUR

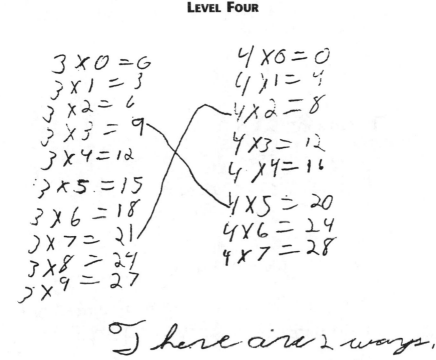

$$3 \times 0 = 6$$
$$3 \times 1 = 3$$
$$3 \times 2 = 6$$
$$3 \times 3 = 9$$
$$3 \times 4 = 12$$
$$3 \times 5 = 15$$
$$3 \times 6 = 18$$
$$3 \times 7 = 21$$
$$3 \times 8 = 24$$
$$3 \times 9 = 27$$

$$4 \times 0 = 0$$
$$4 \times 1 = 4$$
$$4 \times 2 = 8$$
$$4 \times 3 = 12$$
$$4 \times 4 = 16$$
$$4 \times 5 = 20$$
$$4 \times 6 = 24$$
$$4 \times 7 = 28$$

There are 2 ways.

This response not only offers both correct answers but a clear explanation of how those answers were found. It is a weak "4" however, since the student presents no indication of how he or she was sure that all the possible combinations had been found.

LEVEL FOUR

4 wagons - 3 tricycles
            yes
7 tricycles - 2 wagons

I got my answer by multiplying
and guessing. I guessed a number and
multiplied it by 3 or 4 Then I subtrac
that number from 29. If I could
divide that number by 3 or 4 evenly,
then that was one of the combinations.

This response offers a highly systematic approach and both
correct answers to the problem. An explanation of the method
is not presented; however, it was not asked for.

WRITE A STORY

MATHEMATICS STANDARDS ASSESSED

- Number operations and concepts
- Problem solving and mathematical reasoning
- Mathematical skills and tools, and
- Mathematical communication

DIRECTIONS TO THE STUDENT

The equation $4 \times 5 = 20$ may be used as the number sentence for a lot of different stories. For example: "Jessica had four rabbits, and each one of them had five babies. How many baby rabbits did she have?" Write another story that could be expressed by $4 \times 5 = 20$.

Note to the teacher:

Any number sentence, using any operation, may be used for this task. Students should have many opportunities to write stories for different number sentences.

MATHEMATICAL CONCEPT

Many students, while they can solve complex computational problems, do not know the real meaning of the operations. This is evident from their inability to create a story for a simple number sentence. Practice in this area will serve to cement their understanding of the different operations.

Intermediate level students can benefit from creating stories using subtraction. When given a number sentence such as "8 - 5 = 3", most students will write a story involving removal of some kind; "Charlie had 8 pieces of candy and he ate (or gave away) 5 of them. How many did he have left?" Students should be encouraged to incorporate other subtraction concepts, such as comparison, into their subtraction stories.

In addition, many students will write a situation for a number sentence, but forget to write the question. A story is not complete without the question.

SOLUTION

There are many possible correct stories that will fit any given number sentence.

SCORING GUIDE

	Level One	Level Two	Level Three	Level Four
Completeness	Story not complete; missing an essential element.	Story almost complete; may be missing only a minor element.	Story complete; no elements missing.	Story complete; no elements missing.
Quality	Story does not reflect the operation asked for in the problem.	Story partially reflects the operation asked for in the problem.	Story completely reflects the operation asked for in the problem.	In addition, the story is imaginative and engaging.

Appendix

Student Hand-Outs

Please feel free to photocopy the material in this Appendix
and distribute to your students.

DICE TOSS

Name _____

Directions:

William is tossing two number cubes, each with the numbers 1 through 6. He has bet his friend Tony that if they each toss the cubes the same number of times he can toss a "7" more times than Tony can toss a "5." Tony has asked for your advice as to whether he should accept the bet. What do you think? Write him a short letter explaining why he should or should not accept William's bet, and why.

DOG FOOD

Name _____

Directions:

Kathy's family has two dogs, Charlie and Spot. Charlie is a big dog and eats a whole can of dog food each day. Spot is smaller and eats only 2/3 of a can each day. If dog food costs $2.00 for three cans, how much will it cost Kathy's family to feed the dogs each month (30 days)? You may draw pictures to assist you.

Show your work clearly, so another person could tell how you arrived at your answer.

186

FENCING

Name _____

Directions:

You work for a fencing company that has been asked to prepare an estimate for a job. You use fencing in 4 foot lengths, with two rails and fence posts holding the rails (see the drawing below.) You have been asked to build a fence for a farmer to enclose a rectangular field for cows. The field has dimensions of 600' x 300'. How many fence posts and rails will you need for the job, if the fence were built without a gate? You may use a calculator if there is one available. Prepare a summary of the requirements for fencing material, to present to the president of the company.

As an extension, can you write a rule for determining, for any length of fence, how many rails and posts you would need?

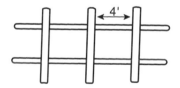

FLOWER PLANTING

Name _____

Directions:

In your town, a group of citizens has decided to make a huge circular flower bed in the center of town, and they have been planting bulbs in the bed. The drawing below shows where the bulbs have already been planted, and they need your help in determining how many more bulbs to buy. They have already planted about 4000 bulbs.

Determine how many more bulbs they will need to complete the flower bed, and write a brief description of how you found your answer.

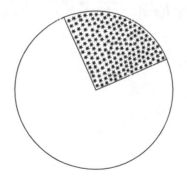

FRACTION FACTS

Name _____

Directions:

Below are five fractions:

$$\frac{1}{4} \qquad \frac{1}{3} \qquad \frac{1}{9} \qquad \frac{1}{2} \qquad \frac{1}{12}$$

1. Write the fractions in order from smallest to largest.

2 Jose told Chris that for fractions with a "1" in the numerator - the top, the larger the number in the denominator - the bottom - the smaller the fraction. Is Jose correct about this? How do you know?

GARDEN FENCE

Name _____

Directions:

Elizabeth has decided to plant a rectangular flower garden with 24 plants. The plants need to be 1 foot apart. She also knows that the rabbits like to eat young plants, so she has decided to put up a fence around her garden.

Elizabeth does not want to buy more fencing than she has to, and she thinks it might matter how she plants the garden. What do you think? How should Elizabeth plant her garden so she needs the least amount of fencing? Show your answer in pictures and in words.

MAKE A NUMBER

Name _____

Directions:

How many ways can you make 25? Use all the operations you have learned.

MAKING CHANGE

Name _____

Directions:

Lynn had only quarters, dimes and nickels to buy her lunch. She spent all her money and received no change. Could she have spent $1.98? Explain how you know.

OUTFITS

Name _____

Directions:

Maria is going to visit her cousins for the weekend. She packs a pair of purple pants, a pair of jeans, and a pair of blue shorts. For shirts she takes a blue tee-shirt, a white tank top, a yellow blouse, and a green shirt. How many different outfits can she make?

A picture or table will help you to organize the information.

Write a description of how you figured out your answer.

PACKING TAPE

Name _____

Directions:

Your family is moving to a new house, and you are helping with packing your belongings. You and your family have decided that you will have 75 boxes to move; your mother has asked you to buy tape to close the boxes.

When you ask your mother how much tape to buy, she answers: "The boxes are 24" long, 18" wide, and 16" high. The boxes should be taped one time all the way around lengthwise. To make sure the boxes are secure, you will also need to put three strips of tape across the top."

How much tape will you need to do the job?

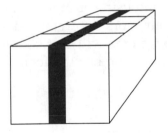

At the store, you find the following prices for tape:

> 50 yards @ $.99 per roll
> 100 yards @ $1.89 per roll
> 200 yards @ $3.29 per roll

How many rolls of each size will you buy, and what will be the total cost? Explain how you made your decision.

PARTY PLANNING

Name _____

Directions:

For your birthday you have invited five friends to your house for snacks and to watch a movie. Your mother has given you $13.00 to spend for the evening. You know that the movie rental is $4.00, and you can choose what to buy for the snacks. However, your mother has promised the other parents that **at least two** of the snacks will be **healthy foods.**

Decide what to buy for your party, using the prices, making reasonable estimates of how much of each item your friends will want.

Make a list, with quantities, to show your mother, indicating how much it will cost, and using as much of the money as possible. Try to make your work as organized as possible, estimating how much your items will cost before you add them. You may use a calculator. The healthy foods are marked with an asterisk (*).

Cookies	$2.39
*Six-pack of yogurt	$1.90
Half-gallon of ice cream	$3.89
*Half-gallon of milk	$1.59
Six-pack of soda	$1.79
Large bag of chips	$1.79
*Box of six cheese pizzas	$4.89
*Bag of six oranges	$1.59
Microwave popcorn	$2.39

PARTY PRIZES

Name _____

Directions:

At a party six identical prizes were hidden. Anna and Beth both searched for them until all six were found.

In the table below, list all the different possible numbers of prizes that each girl could have found. One possibility has already been written into the table.

Number of Prizes found by Anna	Number of Prizes found by Beth
0	6

Explain why Beth could not have found exactly one more prize than Anna.

PEANUTS

Name _____

Directions:

The students in Ms. Hartman's class bought some peanuts that come in small bags. Each student in the class reported how many peanuts were in his or her bag. Here are the results:

Number of Peanuts in a Bag

14   17   15 16   16   18   21   13   15   14   15
   15   16   17   17   19   17   16   19   15   19

If someone asked you "About how many peanuts are in a bag?" what would you say? How many possible answers are there? Explain the reasons for your answer or answers.

PET SURVEY

Name _____

Directions:

Which pets do you think are most popular with the families of students in your school? In this problem you will take a survey of students in one class, and compare your results with those of classmates who have surveyed students in another class.

To do this task, you should:

1. design a questionnaire to use with students in another class, to find out how many and what types of pets they have at home

2. survey all the students in the other class

3. summarize your results

4. make a graph of your findings

5. compare your graph with at least one classmate, and

6. write a comparison of the information in your graph with that of your classmate

PIECES OF PIZZA

Name _____

Directions:

Jose ate 1/2 of a pizza. Ella ate 1/2 of another pizza. Jose said that he ate more pie than Ella did, but she said they both ate the same amount. Who do you think is right? Is it possible that neither Jose nor Ella is correct? Use drawings or pictures and words to explain your answer.

PIZZA CHOICES

Name _____

Directions:

The director of your school cafeteria has decided to offer pizza on Fridays, but is not sure what kind to provide. Your class has been asked to help decide.

1. Devise a method to determine what kind of pizza students in another class in the school prefer. Interview or survey students in that class.

2. Summarize, using both words and a graph, the information you have collected.

3. Write a letter to the cafeteria manager, explaining whether you think your survey can serve as the basis for deciding the school's Friday lunch menu.

SALE PRICE

Name _____

Directions:

Brian's bicycle shop had 48 water bottles for sale, but since winter was coming he wanted to sell as many as he could. On Monday, Brian marked the water bottles down to $5.00 each and sold 1/2 of them. On Tuesday, he marked the remaining bottles down to $4.00 each and sold 1/2 of what was left. On Wednesday, he marked the remaining bottles down to $3.00 and sold 1/3 of the remaining bottles. On Thursday Brian marked the remaining bottles down to $2.00 and sold them all.

If Brian paid $4.00 each for the bottles, how much money did he gain or lose in selling these bottles? Explain your reasons.

SCHOOL PLAY

Name _____

Directions:

Tickets to the school play cost $1.00 for students and $2.00 for adults.

1. If $125 was collected, how many adults and how many students could have attended the play? How many different possible answers are there to this question? Find as many as you can.

2. If programs for the play cost $.50 to produce, how much profit would the school make with different combinations of students and adults attending the play? If the school wanted to make as much profit as possible, would it encourage students or adults to attend the play?

3. Write a letter to the play's manager explaining how you think profits can be made as large as possible.

SCHOOL SUPPLIES

Name _____

Directions:

It is almost the end of summer vacation, and time to buy school supplies. You have ads from two different stores showing their prices for different school items. Your cousin has given you $20 to spend, and wants you to find the best prices on the things you need.

School Supplies Needed

4 folders
calculator
lined paper (pack of 200 sheets)
ruler (with both standard and metric units)
set of 24 felt tipped pens
backpack
10 pencils

1. Determine the cheapest source for each of the items on the list of school supplies. Make a list that will tell you which items to buy from each store. How much will you have to spend, and how much of the $20.00 will you have left over?

2. If you have time to go to only one store, which store would give you best value? What would be the cost of all the items on the list, and how much change would you receive from the $20.

Is it worth the trouble to go to both stores? Write a brief note to your cousin explaining why you think it is (or is not) worth the trouble to go to both.

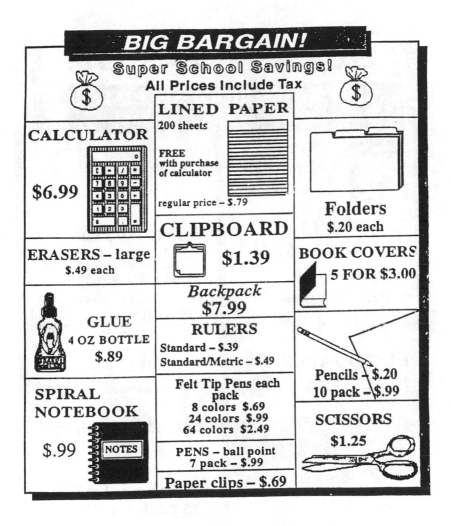

BIG BARGAIN!

Super School Savings!

All Prices Include Tax

CALCULATOR

$6.99

LINED PAPER

200 sheets

FREE with purchase of calculator

regular price – $.79

Folders
$.20 each

ERASERS – large
$.49 each

CLIPBOARD   **$1.39**

BOOK COVERS
5 FOR $3.00

GLUE
4 OZ BOTTLE
$.89

Backpack
$7.99

RULERS
Standard – $.39
Standard/Metric – $.49

Pencils – $.20
10 pack – $.99

SPIRAL NOTEBOOK

$.99   NOTES

Felt Tip Pens each pack
8 colors $.69
24 colors $.99
64 colors $2.49

PENS – ball point
7 pack – $.99

Paper clips – $.69

SCISSORS
$1.25

SUPER VALUE

BACK TO SCHOOL SPECIALS!!!
ALL PRICES INCLUDE TAX

SPIRAL NOTEBOOKS
$.89 each

SCISSORS–$.99

FOLDERS
4 FOR $1.00

Felt Tip Pens
8 colors–$0.60
24 colors–$0.78
64 colors–$1.10

PENS–erasable
5 pack – $1.25

PENCILS–$.69 each
5 pack–$.99

LINED PAPER
200 SHEETS–$.79

RULERS
Standard – $.59
Standard/Metric – $.69

SCHOOL BACK PACK
$9.99

Pencil Sharpener
$.99

BOOK COVERS
Buy 4 get one free
$.69 each

ERASERS–LARGE
3 pack for $1.59

1/2 off special
ABC Calculator–regular price $8.00

SCIENCE FAIR

Name _____

Directions:

Three elementary schools are planning a science fair, which will be held in a multi-purpose room of one of the schools. Space in the multi-purpose room will be allocated to each school according to the number of students in the school: the more students, the more space given to that school.

Jackson School has about 500 students. Kennedy School has about 200 students. Martin Luther King School has about 300 students.

The rectangle below represents the multi-purpose room where the science fair will he held. Show the amount of space each school should get based on each school's population. Label each section J for Jackson School, K for Kennedy School, and M for Martin Luther King School.

Write a description of how you decided to divide the space. How do you know it is fair?

SPINNING ADVANTAGE

Name _____

Directions:

You and a friend are playing a game, using the spinner below. One of you gets a point every time the spinner lands on an odd number; the other gets a point when it lands on an even number. The first person to reach 21 points wins the game. Would you prefer to get the point for the odd or even numbers? Why? Explain why you think that would be better.

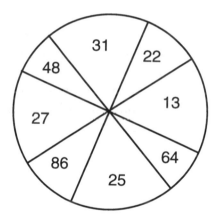

VENDING VALUE

Name _____

Directions:

Carlos wants to buy a 75-cent snack from a vending machine. The machine accepts only nickels, dimes, and quarters. Carlos has 7 nickels, 5 dimes, and 2 quarters.

1. What are all the possible ways that Carlos could pay for the snack? You may use words or pictures.

2. Which of your ways would use the fewest number of coins? Explain why this is so.

WHEELS

Name _____

Directions:

Toni and her friends take their tricycles and wagons to the playground. If Toni counted 29 wheels, how many tricycles and how many wagons were at the playground?

Is there another possible combination of wagons and tricycles? Show how you got your answers.

WRITE A STORY

Name _____

Directions:

The equation 4 x 5 = 20 may be used as the number sentence for a lot of different stories. For example: "Jessica had four rabbits, and each one of them had five babies. How many baby rabbits did she have?" Write another story that could be expressed by 4 x 5 = 20.